T0338987

Ministers of Reconciliation

Preaching on Race and the Gospel

Ministers of Reconciliation

Preaching on Race and the Gospel

Daniel Darling, Editor

LEXHAM PRESS

Ministers of Reconciliation: Preaching on Race and the Gospel

Copyright 2021 The Ethics and Religious Liberty Commission

Lexham Press, 1313 Commercial St., Bellingham, WA 98225
LexhamPress.com

Print ISBN 9781683594772
Digital ISBN 9781683594789
Library of Congress Control Number 2020951821

Lexham Editorial: Elliot Ritzema, Claire Brubaker, Kelsey Matthews
Cover Design: Brittany Schrock
Typesetting: Justin Marr

Contents

Russell Moore

Foreword

Several years ago, reading a Baylor University Press compilation of sermons and speeches from the Jim Crow era, I was struck by one from a pastor, Robbins Ralph, who spoke pointedly to his congregation of the sinful hypocrisy of claiming to follow Christ while remaining silent in the face of white supremacy. "I beg your pardon if I have spoken in such a way as to disturb your thinking," the pastor said at the conclusion of his sermon. "I beg God's pardon if I have not."[1]

This is an important word. As I was writing this, I heard a Christian minister say that questions of racial justice and reconciliation are "perilous waters." Indeed they are, at least once one says anything beyond the most general of platitudes. That is hardly surprising since it is controversial, too, to preach against anything more specific than "immorality" to people who are intent on continuing in sexual sin or murder or theft.

The implication behind those fearful of addressing such questions—whether of human slavery in the 1850s, lynching murders in the 1920s, Jim Crow in the 1950s, or questions of ongoing racism, both personal and systemic, now—is that they should be avoided because they are "controversial." And yet

---

1. Davis W. Houck and David E. Dixon, eds., *Rhetoric, Religion, and the Civil Rights Movement 1954–1965, Volume 1* (Waco, TX: Baylor University Press, 2006), 149.

Jesus inaugurated his own ministry talking about these matters—by pointing out that God's purposes extended beyond Israel to the widow of Zarephath and to Naaman the Syrian, knowing that the crowd would turn from wonder to rage (Luke 4:25–28).

The apostle Paul argued that the union of Jew and Gentile in Christ was a key aspect of the mystery of Christ in the gospel (Eph 3:4–6; Col 3:11), and was willing to confront head-on the apostle Peter when Peter was refusing to be seen eating with Gentiles (Gal 2:11–14). And the New Testament—in continuity with the Law and Prophets long before—affirms that people will be held accountable for unjust practices and systems (Luke 3:12–14; Jas 5:1–6). Racism and racial injustice not only hurt vulnerable people (although that's certainly the case), but also send people to hell. We have no option to overlook sins for which Jesus died. To do so distorts the gospel—and also holds back the word of reconciliation with God for those in need of repentance.

This book includes reflections from many who have taught and preached on these matters, and these essays may well spark within you ideas for how to stand for Christ on these issues in your church or family or community. I am sure that the authors of this book would beg your pardon if your thinking is disturbed, and would beg God's pardon if it is not.

Are these perilous waters? Sure. The Red Sea, the Jordan River, every baptismal pool that joins a follower of Christ to his Lord in crucifixion, burial, and resurrection—these are all perilous waters, too.

Let's follow Jesus there.

1 | Matthew D. Kim

Preaching on Race in View of the Image of God

Genesis 1:27

Race and ethnicity are taboo subjects in many pulpits across the United States. Knowing that some of their congregation will see it as "liberal" talk, a social gospel incongruous with the true gospel, or a ploy of the political left's agenda, many pastors shy away from teaching and preaching on the issues of race and racism—regardless of their rationale for such avoidance. Two camps emerge out of this salient concern. The first camp wonders why we are still needing to talk about race, while the second camp is exhausted by having to explain to the other why discussions on race and racism are essential.

The current climate of anxiety, suspicion, hostility, and even angst makes race and racism particularly ripe topics for conversation in the church. In the spring and summer of 2020, after the murders of Ahmaud Arbery, Breonna Taylor, and George Floyd, books on race were flying off the shelves as many congregations in our country and around the globe tried to make sense of the heinous debacle that we found ourselves in.[1] As a pastor,

---

1. See, for example, Robin DiAngelo, *White Fragility: Why It's So Hard for White People to Talk about Racism* (Boston: Beacon, 2018); Ibram X. Kendi, *How to Be an Antiracist* (New York: One World, 2019); Eric Mason, *Woke Church: An Urgent Call for Christians in America to Confront Racism and Injustice* (Chicago: Moody, 2018);

you may be wondering, "Where do we begin?" and "How can my church's leadership equip and encourage our congregants to act in this turbulent season?" I would suggest that you begin these conversations with a Scripture text that is found in a very early part of the story of God. In order to move forward in our personal and corporate understanding of race and racism, and to clarify the actions we should take, we must properly exegete the concept of the image of God.

PERSONS MADE IN GOD'S IMAGE

While Genesis 1:26 is where the concept of the image of God is introduced, the focus of this chapter will be on 1:27. In his commentary on Genesis, Kenneth A. Mathews explains that this verse is a poem that consists of three lines. The first two lines are arranged in a chiasm (inverted repetition), and the last line explicates the first two:

a **So God created man** *in his own image*
b *in the image of God* **he created him**
c male and female he created them[2]

The Hebrew prepositional phrase translated "in his own image" in 1:27a, *betsalmo*, is used in the third person, indicating that God is speaking about himself. The second prepositional phrase, *betselem* (1:27b), is general and thus translated "in the image of God." Verse 27c adds that God is the creator not just of males in his image, but of both males and females. When God had spoken the universe into existence—with its galaxies, solar

---

Sarah Shin, *Beyond Colorblind: Redeeming Our Ethnic Journey* (Downers Grove, IL: InterVarsity Press, 2017); and Jemar Tisby, *The Color of Compromise: The Truth about the American Church's Complicity in Racism* (Grand Rapids: Zondervan, 2019).

2. Kenneth A. Mathews, *Genesis 1–11:26*, New American Commentary (Nashville: Broadman & Holman, 1996), 172.

systems, planets, land, sea, sky, and all living creatures—he still wanted something more to inhabit this world. For this reason, humankind constitutes the pinnacle of creation. The *NIV Zondervan Study Bible* explains the creation of humankind in these verses as the "last act of God's creative work," which "is the climax."[3] Mathews adds: "The crown of God's handiwork is human life."[4] As beautiful as all the wonders of the world are, God's greatest delight is in the creation of human beings. But what does it mean for men and women to be created "in his own image" or "in the image of God"?

Many scholars have grappled with this mystery. Old Testament scholar M. Daniel Carroll R. has helpfully put these into three different categories, which have to do with "what [humans] inherently are, their potential relationship with the Creator, and their capacity and privilege as rulers."[5] What these categories have in common is that they underscore "the particular value of all persons."[6] This value is accompanied by the role of stewards. God delegated responsibility to Adam to cultivate and take care of the garden of Eden (2:15), even tasking him to name all of the living creatures (2:19–20). Stated another way, Michael S. Heiser observes: "Humanity is tasked with stewarding God's creation as though God were physically present to undertake the duty himself."[7]

---

3. See note on Genesis 1:26–27 in *NIV Zondervan Study Bible*, ed. D. A. Carson (Grand Rapids: Zondervan, 2015), 27.

4. Mathews, *Genesis 1–11:26*, 160.

5. M. Daniel Carroll R., *Christians at the Border: Immigration, the Church, and the Bible* (Grand Rapids: Baker Academic, 2008), 67. See also Matthew D. Kim, *Preaching with Cultural Intelligence: Understanding the People Who Hear Our Sermons* (Grand Rapids: Baker Academic, 2017), 104, 109.

6. Carroll R., *Christians at the Border*, 67.

7. Michael S. Heiser, "Image of God," in *Lexham Bible Dictionary*, ed. J. D. Barry et al. (Bellingham, WA: Lexham Press, 2016).

In New Testament terms, the image of God refers specifically to the incarnate Jesus Christ, to whom Paul refers in 2 Corinthians 4:4 ("Christ, who is the image of God") and Colossians 1:15 ("The Son is the image of the invisible God").[8] The example of Jesus shows the rest of us what it truly means to image God. As Heiser continues,

> Paul writes that believers are destined to be conformed to the image of God's son, Jesus Christ (Rom 8:29). This language is a call to act as Jesus would—to live like him. Acting like Jesus points to the functional idea of the image of God; it suggests we think of the image of God as a verbal idea. By "imaging God," we work, serve, and behave the way God would if He were physically present in the world. In Jesus, God was physically present. Thus, we are to imitate—or, image—Christ.[9]

Through active participation, New Testament Christians are to imitate Christ as God's representation, and thereby become more fully the image bearers of God we were created to be.

DISORDERED DOMINION

Before looking at how to apply Genesis 1:27 in preaching, let us explore what has happened to the image of God in light of the fall in Genesis 3. Mathews points out the popularity of the view that the damaging of the image has affected our ability to rule over creation: "During this latter half of [the twentieth] century the dominant interpretation [of the image], though not new (e.g., Chrysostom), has become the 'functional' one, that the 'image' is humanity's divinely ordained role to rule over the

---

8. Scripture quotations in this chapter are from the New International Version.

9. Heiser, "Image of God."

lower orders (1:26, 28)."[10] In other words, the fall has made us inclined to misunderstand/misapply/misuse our God-given ability to rule and have dominion over creation.

After the fall in Genesis 3, human beings have attempted in their sinful state to continue to rule and to even have dominion over fellow human beings. That is, after Adam and Eve sinned, our sinful nature corrupted the mandate to rule over the creation by usurping God's power in an attempt to control other people. The evidence of seeking control, power, rule, and dominion enters the picture in Genesis 4 as Cain and Abel interact with each other. In an act of rage stemming from jealousy, Cain plots and leads his brother to the field where he murders him. Why? Because God favored Abel's offering more than his.

Cain's responsibility in Genesis 4:2 is to "work the soil," or to cultivate the ground and thereby produce crops. That is his job description. Abel's job is to keep the flocks and raise the animals. When they both give offerings to God, God is less pleased with Cain's because he fails to give God his best work. The problem is not the gift, but the giver. Seeing God appreciate Abel's offering more, Cain becomes angry at his brother. In 4:7 God, already knowing Cain's heart, warns him: "But if you do not do what is right, sin is crouching at your door; it desires to have you, but you must master it."

Unable to contain his desires, Cain succumbs to sin in murdering Abel. In doing so, he loses sight of the image of God in his own brother. Now, Cain did not understand the full scope of the image of God that we do after the coming of Jesus, but he must have known at the least that Abel was like him, a valuable person in every way. Cain thus wrongly exercised dominion

---

10. Mathews, *Genesis 1–11:26*, 164–66.

and rule over his brother by taking his very life. He put himself in the place of God—the very thing that his parents did by eating the forbidden fruit of the garden of Eden. Sin begets sin. It's a downward spiral. God knew one sinful thought "crouching at the door" would engulf Cain to the point where he could kill a fellow human being—even his own brother. Marred by sin, Cain no longer saw the image of God in Abel. For him, Abel's life had no inherent value. His envy and anger led to his determination to jettison even basic human dignity, human worth, and respect for life itself.

Cain's killing of Abel in Genesis 4 can be seen as an undermining of the concept of the image of God in Genesis 1:27 in terms of humanity's ability to rightly rule over creation. If that is the case, how does the misuse of God's dominion and rule express itself in society and in the church? And how can we preach and teach on the healing of the image of God today? This leads to our final conversation point on race/racism and the image of God in terms of our current circumstances.

THE IMAGE AND RACISM

There are many sins that arise from disregarding the image of God, but the particular sin that we are considering in this chapter is racism.[11] Racism is an aberration from God's desire for all human beings to "reach unity in the faith and in the knowledge of the Son of God and become mature, attaining to the whole measure of the fullness of Christ" (Eph 4:13). It is an attempt by one ethnic group to have dominion over another. While there are legitimate positions of authority in human society, such as elected government officials or church leaders, God never

---

11. While there is not space to consider them all, related to racism are the concepts of ethnocentrism, xenophobia, bigotry, and more.

intended for people to have dominion over others. Only God is in the position to have dominion over us all. Racial prejudice has been defined by Scott B. Rae as "negative stereotyping on the basis of race and/or belief that particular races/ethnicities are inferior to others. Racism is the combination of racial prejudice and the institutions of power in any given culture that enable a group to perpetuate patterns of discrimination. ... However, no one's race exempts them from holding immoral racial prejudices."[12] Similarly, in *The Color of Compromise*, Jemar Tisby writes, "Racism can operate through impersonal systems and not simply through the malicious words and actions of individuals. Another definition explains racism as *prejudice plus power*. It is not only personal bigotry toward someone of a different race that constitutes racism; rather, racism includes the imposition of bigoted ideas on groups of people."[13]

Rae and Tisby show us that racism and racial prejudice occur at both the individual and systemic levels. On a systemic level, "*prejudice plus power*" involves the concept of "white privilege [which] often refers to the advantage that comes with being in the majority. It refers to not having to be conscious of one's ethnicity and to the majority culture being seen as the norm. It brings advantage because the majority tends to be respected and trusted in ways that minorities often are not."[14] We should view racism and racial prejudice not just as seeing others as inferior, but also as seeking to preserve a system in which the dominant culture holds power and sets the norms.

Since many who will be reading this book will no doubt come from the dominant culture, I want to state clearly that I

---

12. Scott B. Rae, *Moral Choices: An Introduction to Ethics, 4th ed.* (Grand Rapids: Zondervan, 2018), 441–42.

13. Tisby, *Color of Compromise*, 16.

14. Rae, *Moral Choices*, 435.

am not finger pointing here. As Rae notes, all human beings are susceptible to the sin of racism. In my worst moments, I confess that I have exhibited racism and racial prejudice toward others.[15] We all have, even if we don't care to admit it.

Let me conclude with two practical ways by which you can celebrate the image of God in every person and fight the sin of racism.

CELEBRATE THE IMAGE OF GOD IN EVERY PERSON

The doctrine of the image of God teaches us that all people have inherent value, worth, and dignity in God's eyes. No person is worth more or worth less. Regardless of color, race, ethnicity, gender, and other possible human distinctions, every person deserves respect and equal treatment by virtue of being made in God's image. How we celebrate the image of God will look differently in each ecclesial context, but one practical way to celebrate the image of God in every culture is, as you preach and lead worship, not to draw attention to a person's race/ethnicity in the first or even subsequent visits. Oftentimes, if our churches are homogeneous, we may be overly excited to have visible minority visitors. From the pulpit, we may unknowingly put them on the spot. Years ago, a well-meaning pastor had my wife and I stand up in the middle of the sermon and had everyone clap for us because we were Asian Americans and different from everyone else. It was so awkward. It was a moment of shame and not celebration.

---

15. Read about some of my struggles with racism and racial prejudice in Kim, *Preaching with Cultural Intelligence*, 95–125; and my article, "Preaching in the Period of Pandemic and Prejudice," *Journal of the Evangelical Homiletics Society* 20.2 (Sept 2020): 15–23.

Instead, welcome visitors as human beings made in the image of God, not just as visible/racial minorities. There is a marked difference. When we accentuate differences such as being a visible minority from the outset, we draw unnecessary attention to that difference. Most visible minorities in America live with a daily sense of shame.[16] This is a shame derived from always being reminded that they are not one of "us" (a member of the dominant culture). Most of the world lives according to this honor-shame worldview.[17] As soon as you mention your visitors/listeners being a visible minority or speak to them in a language other than English, they are likely to shut down emotionally. Now, they are internalizing feelings of shame for who they are rather than experiencing the joy of worshiping God in community. There will, hopefully, be a time and place to preach about racial/ethnic differences and engage in racial reconciliation, but their initial visits are not the most opportune time.

FIGHT AGAINST RACISM IN YOUR CHURCH

In order to fight the sin of racism in our congregations, we must be willing to get uncomfortable by naming and acknowledging sin. It is easy to speak against racism theoretically. Most of your church members will say that they are not racists, but you must go deeper and get practical. I think, for example, of the numerous hate crimes against Asian Americans as a result of the COVID-19 crisis. On July 2, 2020, CBS News documented over twenty-one hundred reported cases of such crimes since the pandemic struck.[18] If we are content in saying, "I wasn't

---

16. See Jayson Georges and Mark D. Baker, *Ministering in Honor-Shame Cultures: Biblical Foundations and Practical Essentials* (Downers Grove, IL: IVP Academic, 2016).

17. Georges and Baker, *Ministering in Honor-Shame Cultures*, 19.

18. Erin Donaghue, "2,120 Hate Incidents against Asian Americans Reported during Coronavirus Pandemic," CBS News, July 2, 2020, https://www.cbsnews.com/news/anti-asian-american-hate-incidents-up-racism/.

directly involved in any of these incidents," or, "Well, at least Asian Americans are considered 'model minorities' and they don't have to worry about being killed like black and brown people do," we are only exacerbating the problem. We have to recognize that racism is racism, and when we minimize it or fail to address it head-on, we are prolonging its success.

CONCLUSION

As pastors and preachers, we must not ourselves, and we must not let our congregations, be content to pat our backs because we are not actively part of the problem. We must be proactive in fighting the sin of racism against all people of all skin colors and races, thereby celebrating the image of God in all people. Prayerfully consider preaching on Genesis 1:27 and the image of God to confront the sin of racism as we ask ourselves and our listeners what our attitudes are toward those who are different from us. Challenge your listeners to confess the sin of racism particularly when we view others as being made less than in the full image of God.

Therefore, preach on the image of God, racism, ethnocentrism, and prejudice when the text calls for it. For instance, when preaching and teaching on Acts 15 and the Council of Jerusalem narrative, not addressing ethnocentrism would mean failing to address the crux of the passage. Tackle ethnocentrism and/or racism straight on. As you preach and teach regularly on racism and on the image of God, include moments in the worship service where the sin of racism/prejudice is confessed publicly and regularly. Have prayer meetings with racism as a central concern. Ask for forgiveness as the Spirit of God convicts you, and confess that sin to others directly. Provide spaces for members of visible minority cultures to lament and mourn. Empathize with the pain of your minority listeners. Encourage your listeners to join nonviolent, public gatherings in support of racially marginalized groups. Preach on how Christians should oppose policies that promote racial injustice and inequality. Use more illustrations that celebrate people of color and their contributions to society and to the kingdom of God. Express to your listeners regularly from the pulpit how much you love them and care for them, and so much more. As we engage and lead our congregations to fight against racism in our preaching, teaching, and ministry service, we celebrate the image of God in all persons—to the glory of God.

Known, Seen, and Designed by God

Psalm 139

Every January, around the third week, churches all across the country stop and mark a somber but important occasion: Sanctity of Life Sunday. This is a lament and call to action in response to the tragic, landmark 1973 Supreme Court Decision *Roe v. Wade*, which legalized abortion in all fifty states.

When I was a senior pastor, my go-to passage on this occasion was Psalm 139, written by King David. These oft-quoted words remind us of the value of life at the earliest stages: "You knitted me together in my mother's womb" (Psalm 139:13).[1] It's an important and powerful reminder of how God views unborn life that demands a response from the people of God to stand up for babies in the womb.

But January also holds another significant reminder about human dignity: Martin Luther King Jr. Day. This occasion demands as much lament and call to action as our pro-life witness. And I have found that Psalm 139 can have a similar application to racial justice and racial reconciliation.

---

1. Unless otherwise noted, Scripture quotations in this chapter are from the English Standard Version.

A GOD WHO KNOWS

Psalm 139 opens with a powerful statement: at the earliest stages of life, human beings are seen by their Creator. Consider the language David uses about God's omniscience:

> O LORD, you have searched me and known me!
> You know when I sit down and when I rise up;
>   you discern my thoughts from afar.
> You search out my path and my lying down
>   and are acquainted with all my ways. (vv. 1–3)

Every person, even among the most vulnerable, marginalized populations, is known by God. We often think about God's omniscience and are nervous—God knows me in my worst moments and sees me in ways nobody else sees me—but we should also take comfort that in a world where maybe nobody knows my name, God does. But imagine if we took the point of view off our own being known and focused on the way God knows others. If I'm known by God, so is my neighbor.

When we think God may know us but not know our neighbors, disaster results. This was behind much of the insidious and wicked teaching of much of the white church during slavery and Jim Crow: the idea that somehow the white race is superior, is normative, that to be white is to be more known by God. In many ways, racism is about power. But even as preachers preached this alternate gospel, the souls of enslaved and segregated populations were known by God.

This is a word for us today. We are tempted to write off racism as ancient history, but, as much progress as we've seen in America, there are still deep pockets of injustice. We are tempted to be willingly ignorant of racial disparities, to ignore the cries of our black brothers and sisters, but we should remember that God knows. And we should work to know by listening to our brothers and sisters and helping bear their burdens.

The powerless and marginalized are known and named by God. This is why we can see, in the book of Revelation, "every tribe and tongue and people and nation" around the throne of God in worship (Rev 5:9 NASB). God is building, in Christ, a new family where there is no partiality in terms of his love, and where those who follow Jesus are given a new name. God knows all human beings, but there is a deeper level of being known by God through faith in Jesus Christ his Son, who reconciles those who believe to their Father.

A GOD WHO SEES

David not only takes comfort in knowing that God knows the most vulnerable, powerless people, but also delights that he was seen by God, even as a preborn child. Injustice happens when those in power refuse to see the powerless. This is the evil at the heart of racial superiority. It refuses to see the full image of God in those who look differently. Sadly, many white Christians have believed and preached that perhaps some races had less than the full image of God and thus didn't deserve full dignity. But the Bible makes no such distinction. Every person who has ever been born is a full image bearer, even after sin entered the world (Genesis 9:6).

Quite often, Martin Luther King Jr. employed this biblical language of human dignity. In a sermon in 1965, he said:

> There are no gradations in the image of God. Every man from a treble white to a bass black is significant on God's keyboard, precisely because every man is made in the image of God. One day we will learn that. We

will know one day that God made us to live together as brothers and to respect the dignity and worth of every man. This is why we must fight segregation with all of our non-violent might.[2]

King understood that the basis for ending racial segregation and supremacy was the Christian principle of human dignity. This is why he stood with striking sanitation workers bearing sandwich-board signs that read, "I am a man." It's an appeal to the powerful white interests: "Can you see me as more than just a body or a cog in the machinery of this industry? Can you see me as a full human being?"

This is what David is saying when he writes:

> Where shall I go from your Spirit?
>   Or where shall I flee from your presence?
> If I ascend to heaven, you are there!
>   If I make my bed in Sheol, you are there!
> If I take the wings of the morning
>   and dwell in the uttermost parts of the sea,
> even there your hand shall lead me,
>   and your right hand shall hold me.
> If I say, "Surely the darkness shall cover me,
>   and the light about me be night,"
> even the darkness is not dark to you;
>   the night is bright as the day,
>   for darkness is as light with you. (Psalm 139:7–12)

---

2. Martin Luther King Jr. "The American Dream," July 4, 1965, The Martin Luther King, Jr., Research and Education Institute, https://kinginstitute.stanford.edu/king-papers/publications/knock-midnight-inspiration-great-sermons-reverend-martin-luther-king-jr-4.

This is a God of the shadows—a God who sees what everyone else ignores, and a God who sees the most vulnerable ("Your eyes saw my unformed substance," v. 16). What we don't see, what our eyes are trained to ignore, God sees. As followers of Jesus, we too should ask the Spirit of God to help those of us who enjoy the privilege of living in the majority culture to open our eyes to the injustices around us, to sensitize our souls toward the places where our eyes have been trained to look away.

DESIGNED BY GOD

David saves perhaps his most poignant language for the way he sees the Almighty as Creator. God not only knows and sees human bodies, but he crafts human bodies with intricate design and care. David describes himself as being "knitted … together" (v. 13) and "intricately woven" (v. 15). This description of God's "fearful and wonderful" creation destroys the idea of racial superiority, for every human being, from every race and tribe, of every color and background and income class, was created with precision and care by the triune God. This language echoes the words of Moses in the creation narrative in Genesis 1 and 2, where the act of forming humans is cause for divine deliberation ("Let us make man in our image," Gen 1:26), and the Creator is seen as reaching down and crafting human bodies from the dust of the ground (Gen 2:7).

Humans—unlike any other act of God's creation—uniquely bear the image of God.[3] Humans are God's prized creation. The various colors and races are not accidental but intentional. Seeing one race as superior to another is an assault, therefore,

---

3. See the chapter by Matthew D. Kim in this volume for more on the image of God in Genesis 1:27.

on God himself. It is to say that God hasn't created the races with care and intention in mothers' wombs. An assault on the image bearer is always an assault on the image giver.

Pastors, in preaching this passage, would do well to apply Psalm 139's rich description of God's care in crafting human bodies in both individual and social ways. Our weary, burden-laden people need to hear that our identities are rooted not in our socioeconomic status or party affiliation or career success but in the truth that each of us was handcrafted by God for his purpose from the very beginning of our existence. And yet our people also need to hear that Psalm 139 is not just a passage for individual identity crises, but should also be the lens by which we see our neighbors. My neighbor was also knit together by a loving God in the womb. So what does it look like to see bodies that look different from us as human beings stitched together carefully and intentionally by God? Psalm 139 means that George Floyd was not a disposable person, but a human being formed by the Almighty at conception. It means the "other" outgroups, the people we are least likely to understand and love, are image bearers of the divine.

A sinful world filled with sinful broken hearts and sinful broken systems pits races against each other in a violent assault on God himself. It is in the gospel where these walls are broken down, and God, in Christ, is in the act of a new creation (Ephesians 2:14–18). He's drawing together, in his body, people from every nation, tribe, and tongue.

This mosaic we see in John's vision of the future kingdom is the fullest expression of the image of God, this mosaic of redeemed people from across the ages and centuries, representing every single people group. We often claim, in a well-meaning attempt at unity, to "not see color," but God sees color. To imagine it away is to not behold God's intricate design described by David. But to see color is to embrace the beautiful kaleidoscope of color in this new kingdom of God. This is what God is doing, this is where we are headed, this is the work of Jesus.

Jeremiah and His Unexpected Rescuer

Jeremiah 38:1–13; 39:15–18

As a pastor there may be times when you would like to address ethnic issues in your sermon, but do it indirectly. For example, one of the misconceptions many of your people may have is that the Bible is a story about white people, or even a story about a mono-ethnic people. It is often helpful as you preach to point out the multiethnic composition of the people of God in the Bible and to underscore the important role that these multiethnic people play. Preaching on Jeremiah 38–39 will introduce your congregation to the dynamic character Ebed-Melek, an African who trusted in God and who rescued the prophet Jeremiah.

HISTORICAL AND
LITERARY CONTEXT

Jeremiah 1 informs us that Jeremiah was called by God around the year 627 BC. The prophet had a long and difficult ministry, preaching for over forty years to kings and people who basically ignored him and his message from God. The events in Jeremiah 38–39 take place toward the end of Jeremiah's career, in 587–586 BC. Jeremiah 37:2 sums up the discouraging situation: "Neither he [King Zedekiah] nor his attendants nor the people of the land paid any attention to the words the Lord had spoken through Jeremiah the prophet."[1]

In spite of Jeremiah's continued warnings, the kings, the officials, and the people of Judah have abandoned the God of Israel to worship idols. Now the time for judgment has come, and, as Jeremiah has foretold, the Babylonian army is at the gates of Jerusalem.

EXEGESIS

In Jeremiah 37 the prophet Jeremiah is arrested. In 37:21 he is confined in the courtyard of the king's guard. In 38:1–3 we learn that Jeremiah has been telling people that the Lord is going to make the Babylonians victorious over Jerusalem (a judgment Jeremiah has been preaching for years), and that if the people in Jerusalem want to survive they need to surrender to the Babylonians. This message was not received favorably by the leaders of Jerusalem, who are trying to rally the soldiers in Jerusalem to stand strong against the Babylonians. These officials go to King Zedekiah and demand that Jeremiah be executed for this. They declare, "this man is not seeking the good [Hebrew *shalom*] of these people but their ruin [Hebrew *raah*]" (38:4). The Hebrew word *raah* is used frequently throughout Jeremiah, both in reference to the sin of the people (often translated as "evil") and to the punishment that God will bring on them (often translated as "disaster" or "ruin"). Ironically, these officials/leaders have it exactly backwards; it is not Jeremiah who will bring *raah* (as in disaster, judgment) on them, but their own disobedient *raah* (wickedness). Only by obeying the word of God given through Jeremiah can they avoid the coming judgmental *raah* from God. Zedekiah acquiesces to their demands and the officials then lower Jeremiah down into an empty but muddy water cistern in the ground, apparently

---

1. Scripture quotations in this chapter are from the New International Version.

assigning him to starve to death here (38:5–6). The reference to using "ropes" implies that the cistern is quite deep. The cistern belongs to "Malkijah, the king's son," implicating the royal family in this terrible plan to let Jeremiah starve to death. Not one person from Judah or Jerusalem defends him or tries to prevent his death.

Indeed, Jeremiah will be rescued by a very unusual and unexpected person, Ebed-Melek the Cushite (38:7–13). Ebed-Melek hears of Jeremiah's plight and quickly approaches King Zedekiah publicly ("sitting in the Benjamin Gate" implies Zedekiah is holding public court). He declares that these officials have acted "wickedly" (the same Hebrew root word as *raáh*) and that Jeremiah the prophet will soon die if left in the cistern. Notice the contrast between how the leaders disdainfully refer to Jeremiah as "this man" (38:4) and how Ebed-Melek respectfully refers to him as "Jeremiah the prophet" (38:9). King Zedekiah quickly agrees with Ebed-Melek, probably implying that the mysterious Ebed-Melek is an influential, powerful person. Then Ebed-Melek moves quickly to retrieve Jeremiah from the cistern, saving his life.

Ebed-Melek's *Cushite* identity is stressed, for it is mentioned four times (38:7, 10, 12; 39:16; see also this word in 13:23). Who were the Cushites, and who is Ebed-Melek? The Hebrew word "Cushite"/"Cush" is used fifty-five times in the Old Testament, almost always in reference to an ancient and powerful African kingdom located along the Nile River just to the south of Egypt. Modern historians often call this kingdom Nubia. The Greeks referred to everything south of Egypt as Ethiopia. Thus the Greek translation of the Bible, called the Septuagint, translated this word as "Ethiopia." Some English translations also use the term "Ethiopia" occasionally to translate the Hebrew word "Cush." Keep in mind, however, that the region referred to here is different from the area occupied by modern Ethiopia. Cush was along the Nile River south of Egypt, in what is now Sudan. Because

Cush had a long, continuous relationship with ancient Egypt, Cushites are frequently depicted in ancient Egyptian art, where they are easily and distinctively recognizable because of their black African physical features. There is no scholarly doubt that Ebed-Melek was a black African.

In Hebrew, the name Ebed-Melek literally means "servant/ slave of the king." Older commentaries on Jeremiah sometimes assume that he was actually a slave of the king, but there is little evidence to support that view and overwhelming evidence against it. Would a slave be able to convince King Zedekiah to reverse a ruling that he had made with the full support of all the leaders in Jerusalem? Not likely. Also, while the term ʿebed by itself can refer to a slave, the phrase ʿebed-melek is used distinctively as a title for high-ranking officials. Numerous ancient seals and seal imprints have been discovered in Israel and surrounding countries that belonged to high-ranking officials referred to as "servant of the king" or "servant of such-and-such king." So Ebed-Melek the Cushite is probably a high-ranking official. The Hebrew term in 38:7 that is sometimes translated as "eunuch" is also used to refer to "officials," and that is probably the meaning of the term here.

The Cushites were also famous throughout the ancient world as soldiers. They were a common and well-known feature of the Egyptian army, but they also sometimes served as mercenaries in other armies (recall the Cushite messenger in King David's army; 2 Samuel 18:19–23). At this time in history, the Egyptians were allied with Judah against the Babylonians (Jeremiah 37:6–7). It is highly probable that Ebed-Melek the Cushite is somehow related to the Egyptian army, perhaps a military attaché of sorts. This might explain why Zedekiah so quickly agrees to Ebed-Melek's request to save Jeremiah. With the powerful Babylonian army at his gates, he cannot risk offending a representative of the Egyptian army, the only possible source of military relief he might receive.

As the story continues in Jeremiah 38–39, the Babylonians do in fact capture and destroy Jerusalem. As Jeremiah had warned, the consequences are terrible for the inhabitants of Jerusalem. The Babylonians burn the palace and the homes in the city. Most of those leaders who sought Jeremiah's execution in 38:4–6 are ironically executed themselves by the Babylonians in 39:6. Recall that Jeremiah had been placed in a cistern owned by one of the sons of Zedekiah (38:6). Here in 39:6 the Babylonians execute all of the sons of King Zedekiah before his eyes, then gouge out the king's eyes and take him in shackles to Babylon. In contrast, Jeremiah survives the destruction of Jerusalem. The Babylonians give him complete freedom to choose what he wants to do and where he wants to live (39:11–14).

Next the text tells us what happened to Ebed-Melek (39:15–18). God declares to Ebed-Melek, "I will rescue you. … I will save you; you will not fall by the sword but will escape with your life, because you trust in me" (39:17–18). Because of his trust in God, he will be saved. The fate of Jeremiah and Ebed-Melek is ironically contrasted with the fate of King Zedekiah and the leaders of Jerusalem, who opposed Jeremiah and denied the word of God. God rescues his prophet Jeremiah and Ebed-Melek, the one who trusted in God, while in judgment handing over Zedekiah the king, the leaders of Jerusalem, and the rest of the inhabitants to the Babylonians. The implications are that being part of the people of God will be based on faith and obedience—not Hebrew ethnicity.

PRINCIPLES TO BE LEARNED

There are many lessons we can take from this passage. One is that God's people should always accept and obey the word of God, even in the face of opposition. Likewise, we should courageously stand up for what is right, based on the word of God, even if no one else does. We should embrace the importance of faith and trust in God, realizing that salvation comes through faith alone. Related, we should acknowledge that disbelief and rejection of God's word result in judgment.

In addition, there are several important truths emerging from this text in regard to race and ethnic issues. Many white Christians assume that the Bible is about people like them—that is, white people. It is important for them to recognize that many of the characters in the Bible were actually Semitic and looked more like today's Middle Easterners than like white Americans. Furthermore, the people of God in the Bible also often reflect a wide ethnic mix. In addition, black Africans like Ebed-Melek play important roles in the Bible. In the book of Jeremiah, this black African is a hero, saving Jeremiah's life and professing faith in God when all of those in Jerusalem reject Jeremiah and the word of God.

Another important lesson comes from exploring the role that Ebed-Melek plays in the theology of the book of Jeremiah. Many of the other prophets, especially Isaiah, speak of a coming future deliverance of the gentiles, often referred to theologically as the "gentile inclusion." Instead of referring explicitly to a "gentile inclusion" like Isaiah does, however, Jeremiah instead includes the story of Ebed-Melek to convey the same truth. Indeed, the faith, courage, and salvation of Ebed-Melek represents in narrative form what Isaiah is proclaiming poetically in his prophecies—that gentiles will be truly saved and incorporated into the people of God. In today's context in which white Christians often assume that black people were, at best, added late in the history of Christianity, it is significant to note that Jeremiah uses a black African to be the representative of the future salvation for gentiles (which would include the salvation of white Christians today).

It is also very interesting to note the numerous similarities between the story of Ebed-Melek the Cushite in Jeremiah 38–39 and the story of the Ethiopian eunuch in Acts 8:26–40. Recall that the Greek term "Ethiopia" does not refer to modern Ethiopia, but rather to black Africa in general and often to the region occupied by the modern country of Sudan in particular. The mention in Acts 8:27 of Queen Kandake connects this man to the ancient region of Cush. That is, Ebed-Melek in Jeremiah and the Ethiopian eunuch in Acts 8 are from the same place. Both of them are black Africans. More importantly, they both come to true faith in God at precisely the time when most of the people and the leaders in Jerusalem have rejected God and his message and are actively persecuting God's messengers (see Jeremiah 37; Acts 8:1–3). In the book of Acts, the Ethiopian eunuch is the first gentile to come to faith, and he symbolizes the soon-to-explode gentile inclusion. So in both the book of Jeremiah and the book of Acts, black Africans from the region in Africa just south of Egypt believe the word of God and place their faith and trust in God at exactly the same time as the people and leaders of Jerusalem reject God's message and his messengers. In both the Old Testament and the New Testament, the inspired authors choose to use black Africans to be central paradigms for the gentile inclusion into the people of God.[2]

2. For further reading, see J. Daniel Hays, *From Every People and Nation: A Biblical Theology of Race, New Studies in Biblical Theology* (Downers Grove, IL: InterVarsity Press, 2003), 130–39; Hays, "Central Paradigms for the Gentile Inclusion: An Intertextual Comparison of Jeremiah's Ebedmelech and Luke's Ethiopian Eunuch," *Sapientia Logos* 3.1 (2010): 1–24; Hays, "The Cushites: A Black Nation in Ancient History," and "The Cushites: A Black Nation in the Bible," *Bibliotheca Sacra* 153 (1996): 270–80, 396–409; Hays, "From the Land of the Bow: Black Soldiers in the Ancient Near East," *Bible Review* 14 (1998): 28–33, 50–51; Hays, *Jeremiah and Lamentations*, Teach the Text Commentary (Grand Rapids: Baker, 2016), 272–85.

Race and the Great Commission

Matthew 28:19–20

Our Declaration of Independence puts forth a lofty ideal about the equality of races, one of the most eloquent and profound ever made: "We hold these truths to be self-evident, that all men are created equal." Before the ink on the page was dry, of course, many of its framers had returned home to their slaves.

Though our country has always had high aspirations of equality, we've never quite been able to achieve them. Not during the century of its birth, when imported African slaves were bought and sold as property. Not after the Civil War, when Jim Crow laws kept newly liberated black people from the full rights of citizenship. Not today, when disparities between the experiences of white citizens and people of color in our country still persist despite great effort to remove them.

So while our society recognizes the need for racial reconciliation, it seems to lack the resources to accomplish it. Legendary civil rights activist and preacher John Perkins once told me the United States's laments about race remind him of Paul's words about righteousness in the book of Romans: no matter how eloquently stated, the law is powerless to accomplish those ideals it upholds (Romans 8:3). The law is like the railroad tracks that point us in the direction to go but are powerless to move the freight in that direction.

As with all areas of spiritual maturity, the gospel alone supplies the resources to achieve multiethnic unity. That's why Paul tells us in Ephesians 3:6–10 that a church united in its diversity reveals the wisdom and power of God. Thus, churches that take the proclamation of the Great Commission seriously will seek, in their membership, both to reflect the diversity of their communities and to declare the diversity of the kingdom.

WHY CHURCHES THAT CARE ABOUT THE GREAT COMMISSION PURSUE MULTIETHNIC UNITY

Embedded in the Great Commission itself is a command for believers to be concerned with seeing the gospel advance beyond the borders of their own ethnicity. Jesus says: "Go, therefore, and make disciples of all nations" (Matthew 28:19).[1]

Christians have historically recognized the implications of this verse for world missions but have often ignored the implications for evangelistic work in their own communities. Not only does God call us to reach those parts of our city where people look, think, dress, and vote like us, but he also calls us to those parts of our city where people don't.

Churches that care about evangelizing the United States will increasingly make this a priority. Studies indicate that by 2050, no ethnic group in the United States will comprise a majority.[2] In 2018, the North American Mission Board

---

1. Scripture quotations in this chapter are from the Christian Standard Bible.

2. Jeffrey S. Passel and D'Vera Cohn, Pew Research Group, "U.S. Population Projections: 2005–2050," February 11, 2008, https://www.pewresearch.org/hispanic/2008/02/11/us-population-projections-2005-2050/.

reported that more than 60 percent of all the churches they planted were led by leaders of color. Thus, if we want to reach our cities—reaching all peoples in our cities, not just those who look like us and live near us—multiethnic unity must become a priority.

But does Jesus' command to reach all nations mean simply that we should seek to plant churches among all the nations, or does it hint at multiethnicity within local churches? Should we strive to plant churches in our cities among all the ethnicities, or for churches in our communities that bring the ethnicities of our community together?

The apostles seemed to assume the latter, insofar as that was possible. When Paul, for example, brought the gospel to a new city, he didn't plant a "Jewish church" on one side of the city and a "gentile church" on the other side. He planted one church consisting of Jew and gentile, and a great deal of his instruction to those churches concerned how the gospel had torn down the "dividing walls," overcoming a division and creating "one new man" out of two (Ephesians 2:14–22). The apostle Peter, too, describes the gospel-driven process of building the various races together into a "chosen race" and *one* "holy nation" (1 Peter 2:9, though it seems to have taken Peter longer to get there; more on that in a moment). Every indication from the New Testament letters assumes that these early churches were multiethnic.

Or consider what happened when Paul carried the gospel to Philippi (Acts 16:11–40). We might not register how significant it is that the first three converts in Philippi are a woman named Lydia (16:14–15), a young slave girl (16:16–18), and a gentile jailer (16:25–34). But consider what Jewish rabbis prayed every day: "God, I thank you that I am not a woman, a slave, or a Gentile." Is it any accident that Paul followed God's lead by planting a church in Philippi with ... a *woman*, a *slave*, and a *gentile*? Great Commission evangelism and multiethnic unity have always gone hand in hand.

Furthermore, one of the defining characteristics of the New Testament's most evangelistic church, Antioch, was its multi-ethnic unity. Luke seems to go out of his way to note the different ethnicities of the leaders—with no apparent reason for pointing that out other than to demonstrate that they were different (Acts 13:1). Can it be coincidental that this is the first place the disciples are called "Christians" (Acts 11:26)? It is as if here, in Antioch, the believers began to assume an identity even larger than their ethnicity. Their unity in Christ simply outweighed their distinctions in culture.

I recognize that some churches have greater opportunities here than others. At The Summit Church, where I pastor, we have the benefit of being in the heart of a large, ethnically diverse city. Many churches throughout the United States are in more ethnically monochromatic areas, and they shouldn't be judged too harshly for that. They too must reflect the diversity of their communities, and if their communities are more monocultural, then their churches likely will be also. Furthermore, language barriers might make it more prudent, at least for a time, to conduct services tailored to specific communities. (For example, we have Mandarin services and Spanish services for first-generation immigrants who cannot speak English well enough to participate meaningfully in our English services.) But regardless of our surrounding content, the core principle remains the same: churches that care about the Great Commission must promote multiethnic unity wherever they can. The gospel's aim is to bring together what sin has separated.

THE GOSPEL ALONE EMPOWERS
MULTIETHNIC UNITY

Years ago, I was having breakfast with one of the pioneers of the megachurch movement. His church had exploded in growth based on the "homogeneous unit principle"—the idea that you can reach more people if you aim explicitly for one demographic. His church had reached over twenty-five thousand weekend attenders because he had tailored it for middle class, white suburbanites.

But then he said something that shocked me:

> If I could do it over again, I would pursue racial diversity from the beginning, even if our church was only half the size it is today. Reaching fewer people in *one* church would be worth it, because the corporate witness of racially diverse churches in the United States would be more powerful, and would likely result in a greater total number of conversions than a numbers surge in any one congregation.

A group of twenty-five thousand white people gathering to listen to great music and an entertaining speaker is not really a demonstration of the power of God. It can happen at a Justin Bieber concert. But a group of people who come together around Christ when they have little else in common declares that God has the power to save.

THE GOSPEL CUTS OFF
RACISM AT ITS ROOTS

What is it about the gospel that uniquely empowers multiethnic unity?

First, the gospel deals with racism, prejudice, and privilege at their roots.

Consider Paul's interaction with Peter in Galatians 2.[3] When Paul wants to confront Peter over his racial prejudice—avoiding the gentiles and refusing to even eat with them—he charges Peter with "deviating from the truth of the gospel" (Galatians 2:14). To Paul, the issue isn't primarily that Peter is being divisive; the issue is that Peter has forgotten the gospel. Paul's aim is not merely to curb Peter's behavior but to cut it off at the roots.

All races find their unity in that they have one Creator, God; one problem, sin; one solution, the blood of Jesus; one baptism, Christ's death; one hope, the resurrection of Christ; one fellowship, the Holy Spirit; and one primary love, the God of glory and salvation.

The gospel goes further by subtly undermining the dividing lines by which we classify people. In the gospel, we receive an identity that goes deeper than any of our other cultural characteristics. As Paul says,

> But now in Christ Jesus, you who were far away have been brought near by the blood of Christ. For he is our peace, who made both groups one and tore down the dividing wall of hostility. In his flesh, he made of no effect the law consisting of commands and expressed in regulations, so that he might create in himself one new man from the two, resulting in peace. He did this so that he might reconcile both to God in one body through the cross by which he put the hostility to death. (Ephesians 2:13–16)

No longer is our humanity defined according to societal groupings. In Christ, there are no righteous or unrighteous, rich or

---

3. For a fuller treatment of this passage, see also Jared C. Wilson's chapter in this book.

poor, black or white. Just as we were one in the condemnation of Adam, so we are one in Christ.

Paul saw his new identity in Christ as greater than any of his other identities. In Christ, he says, "There is no Jew or Greek, slave or free, male and female; since you are all one in Christ Jesus" (Galatians 3:28). It's not that these characteristics vanish; it's simply that the reality of who believers are in Christ outweighs what they are in their flesh. In fact, in 1 Corinthians the apostle applies this in an astounding way:

> Although I am free from all and not anyone's slave, I have made myself a slave to everyone, in order to win more people. To the Jews I became like a Jew, to win Jews; to those under the law, like one under the law—though I myself am not under the law—to win those under the law. To those who are without the law, like one without the law—though I am not without God's law but under the law of Christ—to win those without the law. To the weak I became weak, in order to win the weak. I have become all things to all people, so that I may by every possible means save some. (1 Corinthians 9:19–22)

"To the Jews I became like a Jew"? Uhh ... Paul *was* a Jew. So how does a Jew *become* like a Jew to reach the Jews?

If nothing else, it shows us that Paul held his own Jewish culture *so loosely* that he actually had to *readopt* it in engaging with other Jews. He took it off and on like a garment. A truly gospel-loving Christian will do the same.

Paul is not telling Jewish people to become gentiles or gentiles to become Jews; he wouldn't today tell white people to adopt black culture or black people to adopt white culture. He's telling *all* people to be *kingdom* people, cherishing that identity above every other feature that might unite—or divide—us.

THE GOSPEL MOTIVATES US TO BE COMFORTABLE BEING UNCOMFORTABLE

The gospel supplies us with yet another power that enables us to overcome racial disharmony:

The gospel teaches us to subordinate our needs and preferences to the needs and preferences of others.

Most evangelicals now believe in the equality of the races. Yet still, to use the often-repeated words of Dr. Martin Luther King Jr., "Eleven o'clock is the most segregated hour in America."

This persists, I believe, because many majority culture Christians reduce reconciliation down to the elimination of overt displays of racism. This is not the entire work of reconciliation.

For those of us in the majority culture, reconciliation must also include entering into and bearing the burdens of racial minorities, sharing in their struggles as if they were our own. The first step toward entering into the burdens of others is adopting a posture of listening, not talking. If we are serious about discovering blind spots and moving toward racial unity, those of us in the majority culture must commit ourselves to uncomfortable conversations where we seek more to understand than we do to be understood.

Furthermore, it means being willing to open our worship spaces not only to the diversity of races but to the diversity of preferences and perspectives that go with it.

Our brothers and sisters of color have, for years, been pressing through the discomfort of cultural variances; it is time we in the majority culture join them in that effort. We need to get comfortable being uncomfortable.

This comes up, for instance, in conversations about worship styles. Granted, there isn't one "black" worship style, any more than there is one "white" worship style. But white Christians need to recognize that their preferences for worship music are deeply cultural. What is normal for us is ostracizing for many others. The challenge, then, is to release some of our control over these preferences, experiencing some discomfort for the sake of multiethnic unity.

As Vance Pitman, pastor of a large, thriving multiethnic Southern Baptist church in Las Vegas, says,

> The way to know you are part of a multicultural movement is that you at times feel uncomfortable. If you always feel comfortable in your church, then it's probably not multicultural, but multicolored—a main group of white Southerners who expect those of differing backgrounds to reflect white, Southern culture.

This kind of "comfortable-being-uncomfortable" will manifest in varying ways from one congregation to another. Many majority-culture Christians will be surprised how many things they had assumed were racially neutral actually appealed more to one culture than another.

THE GOSPEL PRODUCES
A MULTIETHNIC WONDER
THROUGHOUT THE WEEK

A friend of mine often says, "We don't want to just host multiethnic events; we want to live multiethnic lives." Perhaps Dr. King's evaluation of the most segregated hour in America overlooked an hour that was even more so: between six and seven o'clock every night for dinner. The reason our worship gatherings don't look multiethnic is that our living rooms don't, either.

It's easy to say we want to pursue multiethnic unity, but it's uncomfortable and difficult work. And it requires dedicated intentionality. To have people from diverse backgrounds in our lives. To ask questions and to listen. To humble ourselves and ask forgiveness. But it's worth it—for Jesus' sake, for his church's sake, and for our own.

This is not something we in the majority culture do as an act of grace for others. It is something we do in obedience to God's commands. And it is something we pursue for our own souls, as well.

Neither our obedience to the Great Commission nor our pursuit of multiethnic unity will gain any traction unless they are rooted in intimate, personal connection. Interpersonal connection is more important than developing the right mission strategies. Interpersonal connection matters more than finding a worship style that white, black, and Latino will all like. (Good luck with that.) Interpersonal connection matters more than sounding the right note on social media. If evangelism and justice don't characterize our personal lives, then everything else we do will be hollow.

In the end, God did not call us to put on a multiethnic display on the weekend but to live out a multiethnic wonder throughout the week. When we begin to live multiethnic lives, our events will very naturally take on a multiethnic flavor.

The power to pursue this kind of unity is found only in the gospel. This is where we as Christians can offer something our society can only yearn for. Our society wants us to be aware. At key moments of national tragedy, they want us to interact. But they can't offer a way for us to love each other like family. But we in the church know that we *are* a family—black, white,

Latino, Asian, Arab, and every other ethnic group that God has lovingly created. As the old saying goes, the ground is level at the foot of the cross.

This kind of unity turned heads when Christianity first burst onto the scene in the first century. And if we pursue multiethnic lives, it's going to turn heads today, too.

Building the Temple with Wisdom

John 4

Once upon a time the Wisdom of God built a temple called Earth.[1] In this temple he made a man to "work it and keep it" (Genesis 2:15), but the man failed to do this. As a result, the temple was corrupted and needed to be cleansed, but the man could not cleanse the temple because he was also corrupted. From Genesis 3 forward we are left asking, Who can cleanse the temple and tend and keep it again? Who can make sure the temple would never be corrupted again?

The apostle John picks up the story in John 4, which tells of Jesus meeting the Samaritan woman at the well. Somehow, thousands of years from the beginning, the story got twisted. There were two stories about the temple that caused division among the Jews and Samaritans. That's when Jesus, the Wisdom of God, who was in the beginning and created the earthly temple (Proverbs 3:19), arrived. Jesus came to build the temple and tell the true story of the temple. In John 4, Wisdom teaches us how to *begin building the new temple in both word and deed.*

---

1. For more on creation as a temple, see T. Desmond Alexander, *From Eden to the New Jerusalem: Exploring God's Plan for Life on Earth* (Grand Rapids: Kregel, 2009), 20–30.

SEEING WISDOM IN JOHN 4

In the first chapter of John's Gospel, we learn that even John the Baptist did not recognize Jesus as the Messiah (John 1:30–31). It was through baptism with water that Jesus was revealed to John the Baptist and "revealed to Israel" (1:31). By the beginning of John 4, word has begun to spread around Judea that Jesus' ministry is outgrowing John's ministry. John is a significant figure, and his ministry is held in high regard by the Pharisees, so Jesus' ministry is garnering attention from the Pharisees because of its growth (4:1).

However, this growth causes tension between John's disciples and Jesus' disciples, and also poses a threat to the Pharisees.[2] Jesus decides to go north to Galilee to ease the tension between the two ministries and to escape the focus of the Pharisees, and passes through Samaria along the way (4:3–4). Yet his popularity continues to grow, even among the most unlikely Samaritans. Through Jesus' departure, John is putting the wisdom of God on display. In his departure from Judea, Jesus arrives among a people and reveals the manifold wisdom of God in building a new temple.

In Samaria, Jesus stops in a town called Sychar (4:5). It's a setting filled with history. He sits by Jacob's well, which is located "near the field that Jacob had given his son Joseph" (4:5) after purchasing it from the sons of Hamor (Genesis 33:18–19). Joseph would be buried on this land (Exodus 13:19; Joshua 24:32). As Jesus sits by the well, Mount Gerizim is in plain sight. In the Old Testament, Mount Gerizim is where Moses gives the Deuteronomic blessings (Deuteronomy 11:29; 27:12). These locations have significance and value to both Jews and Samaritans (more on this below). It is on this land that the

---

2. D. A. Carson, *The Gospel according to John* (Grand Rapids: Eerdmans, 1991), 215.

conversation between Jesus and the Samaritan woman begins to take place.

The well is a place of neutrality. However, the relationship between Jews and Samaritans is not a neutral issue, as John notes, "for Jews have no dealings with Samaritans" (John 4:9). There was a long history of strife between the two, and that history led to social division. Jews during Jesus' time would avoid contact with Samaritans because Samaritans were deemed unclean. Further, Samaritan women were considered to be in a state of continual ritual uncleanness.[3] When Jesus sits and talks with a Samaritan woman, he is talking with a person whose present place and style of worship cannot make her clean (4:19–20). Yet through the breaking of ethnic and social barriers, Jesus points her to a place—the new temple—and invites her to be a part of a people who are being made clean and set apart as a "chosen race, a royal priesthood, a holy nation" (1 Peter 2:9).

Jesus breaks many ethnic and social barriers in this passage. He speaks with the woman about theological issues (John 4:7–15), something men would not do during that time.[4] He ask to receive a drink from the woman's hand (4:7). Later, he dwells with the Samaritan people for a few days (4:40). Through these actions, Jesus displays a scandalous wisdom that comes from above (James 3:17). It is a wisdom that does not build barriers of division. It is a wisdom that does not idolize a present people and place, but seeks "the city that has foundations, whose designer and builder is God" (Hebrews 11:10). Jesus is the wisdom of God embodied in John 4. He is the wisdom that

---

3. G. K. Beale and D. A. Carson, *Commentary on the New Testament Use of the Old Testament* (Grand Rapids: Baker Academic, 2007), 438.

4. Beale and Carson, *Commentary on the New Testament*, 438.

lays the foundational work of building a multiethnic temple in the midst of the complexities of ethnic and social division.

BUILDING WITH WISDOM

Jesus is employed in his Father's family business (John 4:36), and the work of the family is to build a multiethnic temple of living stones (1 Peter 2:5). The building of a multiethnic temple in our time includes the work of racial reconciliation. In the passage, Jesus works to reconcile an ancient divide to build a multiethnic temple. Like any good family business, the work of the family is passed down from the father to the son, and the son passes it down to his son(s). Jesus teaches us, his sons, how to work in the family business. Shadowing is one of the best ways to learn any trade or craft, and here John lets us shadow Wisdom at work.

Here I will highlight just a few lessons from John 4 that will help us to begin the work of building a multiethnic temple in the church today. The first lesson Jesus teaches is that the work is elegantly simple: it is to love your neighbor as yourself. The simplicity of the craft does not mean there are no complexities in performing the craft. Nevertheless, it is of utmost importance to remember the work is simple. Wisdom is about doing simple work that results in the most comprehensive and beautiful structure the world has ever witnessed—a multiethnic temple built of living stones.

The second lesson Jesus teaches us about our work is how to get fellow laborers to "the well" (John 4:6), where the work of reconciliation begins. Jesus doesn't provide an explanation for where he is going or what he is doing. He simply goes and does his work. Had he explained to his fellow workers why he was stopping in Samaria, it probably would have deviated from the work more than necessary. There probably was no argument that Jesus could offer that would have caused the disciples to participate in the reconciling act happening at the well. The environment was too toxic. There was true hatred and division among Samaritans and Jews that no argument could change. As a result, Jesus did the work and gave explanation for the work later. He cleverly got his fellow laborers to the well where the work begins.

Getting people to the well takes skill. To begin the work of racial reconciliation in America—which is presently a toxic environment—we would be wise to begin the work without using arguments and titles that have negative connotations. Even the term "racial reconciliation" could trigger negative thoughts. Even having arguments about the need for racial reconciliation, before doing the work of racial reconciliation, can unnecessarily distract from the work. Instead, find ways to get your people to "the well," where the work of racial reconciliation can begin.

The well in John's story is a place where people go to meet a common need and share a common interest. The people going to the well can be different, but it's a place of commonality. There are wells in your context that transcend the current racial divide. People meet at these places by necessity and common interest. For example, schools can be great wells to begin the work of racial reconciliation. There may be schools in your city that struggle financially, with high dropout rates or poor parent-teacher relations, and where students tend to lack the support they need to succeed. In your church, you could acknowledge the common need and interest of everybody having the chance to get a good education—this holds no negative or racial connotations. Your church could provide a support system that helps students in underresourced schools to better succeed. That's a generally appealing objective and mission. Most people would want to help in an endeavor that meets this type of need.

The third lesson is that asking favors from "foreigners" gains us friends. Most people ask a favor from someone they know they can trust, who is competent enough to fulfill the favor. We typically ask favors from our friends and family, not strangers. But in the very act of asking for a favor, something powerful takes place: we acknowledge the value of the other person. Jesus, by asking the Samaritan woman for a drink, was acknowledging her dignity—it's why she's so surprised.

A good way to ask a favor to gain a friend in the area of racial reconciliation is to invite pastors from outside your context to come and preach in your church. Asking for such an honorable favor, for such a noble need, is very dignifying. Your people will be able to hear and see a neighbor from an unacknowledged context. As a result, your people may see and hear a neighbor, gain a friend, and begin to acknowledge their context.

Also, asking pastors to preach could lead to partnerships. Church partnerships from different contexts could lead to people of both congregations entering into their neighbor's world—not merely just crossing paths. Partnerships can also lead to both churches dignifying each other by asking favors from each other. For instance, when either church is putting on an event, the other church could be asked to help in significant ways. It's important that the favors asked are dignifying, not dishonoring. To ask a friend to merely do the dirty work you don't want to do is not dignifying. To build partnerships with churches in a different context, ask dignifying favors of your new friends.

The last lesson Jesus teaches us about our work, as we gain friends, is that we must tell the true story. But this will take its own section to explain.

TELLING THE TRUE
STORY WITH WISDOM

Jesus began the work of reconciliation by telling the true story. Recapturing the sequence of this story will help us grasp how Jesus, Wisdom personified, uses it to begin to build the new temple.

He begins by asking the woman to give him a drink (John 4:7). The woman, staggered by his request, responds to his words as if they are unwise: "How is it that you, a Jew, ask for a drink from me, a woman of Samaria?" (4:9). At this point, John adds a parenthetical explanation: "For Jews have no dealings with Samaritans." The most apparent reason why they have no dealings with one another is the reason presented to us in the passage—Jews and Samaritans worship at different temples (4:20). This parenthetical history is part of the temple theme woven throughout John's Gospel.

It is important to know that John uses this theme to comfort those who are dealing with the trauma from the destruction of their temples.[5] When John wrote his gospel account, the Jewish and Samaritan temples had been destroyed—the Samaritan temple by the Hasmoneans in the second century BC, and the Jewish temple by the Romans in AD 70. The temples were viewed as the hope, heritage, and the cultural centers of both people groups. John's writing provides the reader with hope that Wisdom has arrived to build the true temple by providing the true story.

The Jews believed the temple should reside on Mount Zion. The story they told was that the temple was corrupted by a corrupt priesthood in Shiloh—the original residence of the

---

5. Andreas Köstenberger, *A Theology of John's Gospel and Letters: A Biblical Theology of the New Testament* (Grand Rapids: Zondervan, 2009), 69.

tabernacle (Psalm 78:60). As a result, the temple was relocated and the polity restructured (that is, from judges to monarchy). In Jerusalem, where the monarchy was built, the temple would be built. According to the Jews, God was setting up permanent residence among *his chosen people*—no other nation was included.

The Samaritans, by contrast, believed the temple should reside on Mount Gerizim (the "this mountain" the Samaritan woman refers to in John 4:20). Their story and history of the temple was that Gerizim was the first center of worship in ancient Israel and the last place where the temple would reside.

The debate between the Jews and Samaritans was about where paradise should reside. Both stories acknowledged that paradise must be present among a people and have a geographical location on earth. But the stories disagreed on whom the people should be and where paradise would be located. As a result, both peoples created a history based partially on truth and partially on hubris and hurt. The ancient debate was centered on two stories with a distorted *telos*, or goal.

American church history is similar. There are different people groups with their own histories. Each history, to some degree, tells a different story that divides. Each story is aiming at the same *telos*. However, there is disagreement on what the final temple (paradise on earth) will look like *in the end* and how the living stones are organized *until the end*. Nevertheless, each group is an eschatological people longing for paradise on earth and longing to see the reality described in Revelation 7:9 of "a great multitude that no one could number, from every nation, from all tribes and peoples and languages, standing before the throne and before the Lamb."

Revelation 7:9 gives us a vivid description of the future. It *describes* the work of God, but cannot fully *depict* what it is like.

Each person looks at the portrait painted there with different eyes and imaginations. What one person sees and imagines is not always what another person will see and imagine. We see through a glass dimly. There's no need to force an imagined reality, but there's also no need to forget a very descriptive reality. Our work is to tell the true story and build with what is true in the story.

In John 4, Jesus neither forces nor forgets the true story of the living temple. He vividly *describes* the future reality of the living temple to the Samaritan woman. He tells her the living temple will be the Holy Spirit living in us (4:23–24). She cannot literally see the reality he describes. She can imagine it, but never fully envisage it. She can begin to comprehend it, but never fully apprehend it. No one in that time could have accurately guessed or imagined how the living temple would come to fruition. Neither did they know *exactly how* to bring it to fruition. The description was clear. The depiction was unclear.

The reality of Jesus' description of the living temple came true after his death and resurrection. This living temple did not begin being built on Mount Gerizim or on Mount Zion, but in an upper room. There a group of Galileans would gather, be filled with the Spirit, and begin the work of building a multiethnic living temple. People from all nations, "Parthians and Medes and Elamites and residents of Mesopotamia, Judea and Cappadocia, Pontus and Asia, Phrygia and Pamphylia, Egypt and parts of Libya belonging to Cyrene, and visitors from Rome, both Jews and proselytes, Cretans and Arabians" (Acts 2:9–11), would miraculously hear the true story of the mighty works of God and become living stones. No one could have guessed or imagined, according to the description that Jesus gave to the Samaritan woman, that the multiethnic living temple would begin to be built in such a unique and miraculous way. In the same way, we have in front of us the description of the future that awaits us in Revelation 7:9, but we must rely every moment on Wisdom to get there.

CONCLUSION

In the end, Jesus the Wisdom of God teaches us that relying on our skill and wisdom can only create mere imitations of the miraculous. Whatever we build with our own wisdom and skill is as wood, hay, and straw (1 Corinthians 3:12). It will not last. Yet Wisdom teaches us every skill we need in word and deed. When we work with him, he makes us into skilled craftspeople (1 Corinthians 3:10). He trains us to build with stones that are as "gold, silver, and precious stones"—stones that are diverse and that last. He trains us to build with living stones that build a living temple—something the world has never seen. It is a work that will never perish. It is a rewarding work (1 Corinthians 3:14). My friends, when we build with Wisdom and tell the true story, we witness and participate in the miraculous.

How God Addresses Our Prejudices

Acts 10

On the evening of March 13, 2006, a group of Duke University lacrosse students paid two African American women to strip for them at a party they were throwing. Five minutes into the festivities, one of the strippers abruptly quit and ultimately accused three of the men of rape. Word began to leak out onto the Duke campus and Durham community, and eventually gained national attention. It's easy to see how news of these events would capture our collective imaginations. Wealthy white men, attending one of the most elite universities in the world and playing a sport synonymous with privilege, are accused of raping a black woman of meager means from the poor section of Durham. We've seen this before, haven't we? The wealthy and powerful abusing their position at the expense of the vulnerable and marginalized. By all appearances, this was an open-and-shut case, and in one of America's most startling ironies, the Reverend Jesse Jackson was in lockstep with the white district attorney of Durham County, Mike Nifong, in their joint melodic pleas for justice.

But oh, how we were wrong. Four years later, these young men were declared innocent, and Mike Nifong was disbarred. The DNA evidence didn't match any of the lacrosse players, and the woman who cried "rape" was ultimately revealed to have fabricated the whole thing. We had all been had, hoodwinked, bamboozled. Race can be quite the con artist, aiding and abetting our deepest presuppositions, seducing us to add or subtract value simply by the color of a person's skin. Try as we may, race has attached itself not only to our skin, but to our minds, casting an ever-present shadow and coloring our perceptions. We just cannot seem to get rid of this demonic system predicated on appearances, making deposits and withdrawals in the accounts of humanity. If ever there were the proverbial elephant in the living room of America, it's race. Yet it's here where I'm thankful to God for speaking consistently through his word into these difficult realities. Acts 10 is one such example offering help and hope.

THE INTERSECTION OF
RACE AND GOSPEL

Acts 10 stands at the intersection of race and the gospel. There's just no way to avoid this. Here we have a minority Jew announcing words of hope and freedom in a house filled with powerful, majority-ethnicity gentiles. To avoid the racial realities of Acts 10 in an attempt to "just preach the gospel" is to do an egregious injustice to the text. Yes, our text is concerned with the content of the gospel and its power to save and transform, but at the same time Acts 10 is also concerned with the context in which that gospel is communicated. Luke is drawing us into the stunning power of the gospel to pull together what Scot McKnight calls "The Fellowship of Differents" (the name of his book that deals with issues of ethnicity).

Beauty is often seen in its contrasts. Jewelers get this, which is why they never plop diamonds down on glass countertops. No. Instead, they place them on black velvet cloths so their brilliance can radiate all the brighter. Storytellers also know this truth. Some of the most powerful love stories involve people who should not be together, transgressing lines of class and race. It's Noah and Allie in *The Notebook*. Jack and Rose in *Titanic*. It's the white Joey Drayton bringing home her African American fiancé Dr. John Prentice in the 1967 film *Guess Who's Coming to Dinner*. These stories evoke a visceral reaction in us because they transgress normative cultural lines, expose our biases, and move us to root for the long shot of love.

Of course, there's no more long shot of love than the story of God coming to earth in the person of Jesus Christ, dying for us, and inviting us into relationship with him. Every conversion is a miracle. Kanye West's profession of faith is no more stunning than yours or mine, for in every case it is beyond shocking that a holy God would venture to the other side of the tracks to save and be with us. Charles Wesley understood this. Dumbfounded with such a contrasting love, he dipped his pen in ink and inscribed these words on paper:

> And can it be that I should gain
> An int'rest in the Savior's blood?
> Died He for me, who caused His pain—
> For me, who Him to death pursued?
> Amazing love! How can it be
> that Thou, my God shouldst die for me?
> Amazing love! How can it be,
> That Thou, my God, shouldst die for me?[1]

Charles Wesley and the author of our narrative, Luke, were both awed by a God who would go so far to be with us. But there's more. Yes, Luke is interested in Acts 10 with the long

---

1. Charles Wesley, "And Can It Be That I Should Gain," 1738.

shot of love, the stunning contrast of the gospel as a holy God stoops to lowly humanity and invites them into the greatest love story ever told. But this is not all: there's another contrast, a sociological one, which only aids to illumine the brilliance of the love story—it is God sending a Jew to the home of gentiles to announce this good news. To only preach the former and neglect the latter is to diminish the full force of Acts 10.

A BIT OF POLYESTER: THE MATTER OF RACE

The application of our narrative is both easy and difficult. It is easy in that to talk about the matter of race is not only within the bounds of our passage; it is right in the crosshairs of Luke's intended purpose. But it is difficult because to talk about race at all will demand courage, a prophetic kind of courage that will no doubt upset and even alienate some in your audience. But this kind of courage is necessary to be faithful preachers and practitioners of the Scriptures.

Now, I understand I may have lost some of my readers by even daring to use the word "race." They would say that there is only one race: the human race. But we should remember a basic etymological principle: that words only have meaning within a given framework or context. So when people talk about there only being one race, they are speaking biologically, which I will give them. The problem is that most of our conversations regarding race are *not biological but sociological.* It is in this sense that race tends to be more like polyester than cotton. Cotton is God-made; polyester is man-made. Race, like polyester, is constructed by humankind. It is real, yet fabricated. When the Bible speaks of people groups it uses the Greek term *ethnos,* or what we would call ethnicity, and not race. In other words, God created and is delighted in people groups. But at the same time, God is not the creator of systems that value or devalue based on skin color or ethnic differences. In this sense, ethnicity is cotton (God-made), and race is polyester (man-made, but also real). In emerging America, when cotton was king, the system of chattel slavery necessitated polyester, where humanity decided to use skin color and attach value to it. In a sociological sense, ethnicity is of God, but race is demonic because it assaults the image of God and plagues us to this day. We see it in Durham courthouses and Ferguson streets.

Minorities do not have the luxury of avoiding the problem of race, even in our twenty-first century world. A part of this has to do with the collective psychological damage race has done to people of color (and this damage works the other way among some whites who think more highly of themselves than they ought because of the color of their skin). W. E. B. DuBois famously asked back in 1897: "Between me and the other world, there is ever an unasked question: ... How does it feel to be a problem?"[2]

On cool mornings, I will throw on my hoodie and venture outside. As I walk, it's common to see people, who happen to be white, go to the other side of the street to avoid me. Right or wrong, my assumption is that this is because I am a large black man in a hoodie with his hands in his pockets and walking briskly. I find myself at times chuckling at the irony: while they are walking to the other side of the street, I'm reciting Scripture and praying for things like the multiethnic church to become the new normal in our world. Yes, Dr. DuBois, I know what it feels like to be a problem.

---

2. W. E. B. DuBois, *The Souls of Black Folk* (New York: Oxford University Press, 2007), 1.

THE HEART OF ACTS 10

Peter's problem is that he is trapped in his own biases, a prisoner of his shadow. God understands this, which is why, before God can use him to advance the gospel across ethnic lines, he must first deal with Peter's racism. Seen in this light, we are forced to conclude that the emphasis of much of Acts 10 is on Peter. Before God chooses to save these gentile people, he must first address some things in the Jewish preacher.

We don't have to spend a day in seminary to figure out Acts 10 has forty-eight verses, and it is not until the middle of verse 23 that Peter makes his way to the gentile home of Cornelius. In the first half of the chapter we find Peter staying in the home of Simon the tanner, where he encounters God in a vision in which he is told to eat food at odds with the Jewish dietary laws he has adhered to since birth. In other words, in the first half of our narrative we find God laying Peter bare and turning the light onto the hidden prejudices he had harbored in his heart toward gentiles. Before Peter can open his mouth and talk about the God who saves every ethnicity, he first must meet with God, who challenges him on his elitist attitudes.

I wish God would have done this with Jonah before he walked into Nineveh. Jonah and Peter had a lot in common. Both were dealing with the intersection of the gospel and race, and both were ethnic Jews who were not, shall we say, "woke." They were beyond reluctant. God had to send a storm, lots, and a great fish after Jonah. And Peter engaged in a theological argument with God as to why he could not eat what God had created. Jonah ultimately went to Nineveh, with a stench on both his heart and his body (he had, after all, spent several days inside a fish), and preached, yet at the end of the narrative he is upset that God would save these "undeserving" gentiles. The story ends with God pressing into Jonah's racism.

Jonah shows us it's possible to preach and be prejudiced at the same time. I know this far too well. I experienced racism at my Bible college and failed to deal with the hurt. Instead of allowing myself to be broken, I became hardened and hid my callousness under the veneer of working in an all-black church right after graduation. A few years later, God called me to go to a predominantly white, wealthy church on the other side of town. I walked into that church like Jonah walked into Nineveh. People were helped by my preaching, and many came to Christ, but my heart was bitter.

Those of us who live in America must have the moral integrity to confess that we have been discipled by a system built on the demonic idol of race. This system has formed us more than we would like to admit. But is this not the point of the first half of Acts 10. When Peter is interrupted by God with the plate of nonkosher delicacies, God is holding up a mirror to his heart, confronting his idols and beckoning him to admit his own sinful disposition. Preaching on race takes a deep humility and honesty, one that can only come about from confronting the inner recesses of our hearts. If we don't, we could end up like Jonah—outwardly accurate and inwardly wrong.

COMMUNITY

Acts 10 lays out for us God's blueprint for how he deals with hearts still in the clutches of racism. Yes, this blueprint is for everyone, but the primary recipient of this is the preacher, Peter. In our time, he is represented by you and me, and not so much the people we preach to. God uses *community*, *catalyzing experiences*, and *content* to ready Peter to advance rightly his program of bringing salvation to the world.

We find Peter staying "in Joppa for many days with one Simon, a tanner" (Acts 9:43). A tanner was a maker of leather products. This was no job for a devout Jew, because according to the law, touching dead animals would have made them ceremonially unclean. Not only would Simon have been unclean, but his home would have been unclean. Under the sovereignty of God, Peter is staying in an unclean home. This is not random, but is part of God's plan to ready Peter to walk into another unclean home, one filled to the brim with gentiles. Before Peter can preach to Cornelius, he must first be in close community with Simon the tanner.

As I write, the world is holding its breath for a much-needed vaccine to cure the dreaded coronavirus. Vaccines introduce your body to small doses of the problem, so that you can overcome large invasions of the problem. Peter has a problem—his heart is sick when it comes to gentiles. So what does God do? Before he sends him to a house filled with them, he gives him one very important relationship that will help to vaccinate his heart and ready him to preach and engage the ethnically other with the love of Christ.

We all need the vaccine of community with the ethnically other if we are going to wage war with the cultural idols of race in our hearts. We hurt in isolation, but heal in community. I've seen this powerfully at work in my own life. My bitter, racist, Jonah spirit is being conquered by the vaccine of loving white siblings in Christ. The people at my first church loved me, even when I did not love them. My wife, Korie, and I have dear white friends whom we vacation with, lean into during life's rough seasons, and just live alongside. Whenever I am tempted to fall back into patterns of racist thoughts and actions, God taps me on the shoulder and brings their faces to mind. Their friendship is a vaccination to my sick heart. Preacher, beware of declaring any truth you are not willing to engage yourself. It is paramount that we extol the virtues of multiethnic churches while we are also gathering at dinner tables with diverse groups of people.

CATALYZING EXPERIENCES

Acts 10 is about the methods God uses to address our prejudices toward ethnically different people. Racism must be addressed or it will continue to serve as an impediment to the gospel of Jesus Christ and the advancement of his kingdom. After God gives Peter community by situating him in the home of Simon the tanner, he reveals himself to Peter through a catalyzing experience on the roof.

A catalyzing experience is a benchmark event that profoundly shapes and even reroutes our lives. All throughout the Bible, we see God use catalyzing experiences as a part of his arsenal in shaping his people. The seminal catalyzing experience in the Old Testament was the crossing of the Red Sea, which not only helped to shape the people of God, but also caused fear and dread to fall on other nations. David's killing of Goliath emboldened the nation of Israel. Nebuchadnezzar's hiatus as a wild animal resulted in his praising the Most High God. Daniel's deliverance in the lion's den had a profound effect on the faith and legislature of Darius and his kingdom. Paul's Damascus Road experience changed his life. The cross and empty tomb turned fearful disciples into courageous apostles who, in the words of Muhammad Ali, "shook up the world."

What should not be missed in Peter's catalyzing experience that begins in verse 9 is the location. While Peter may have had reservations and felt uncomfortable being in the home of Simon the tanner, God shows up in that place. Later on, this theme continues as Peter walks into the gentile home of Cornelius. God will show up in that home, too, as the Holy Spirit is poured out, leading some scholars to call this the "gentile Pentecost." The very places Peter may have harbored reservations about, God rushes in and makes himself at home. All of this leads me to ask, Who am I uncomfortable with whom God is at home with? Whom am I avoiding who God wants me to be visiting?

The vision Peter sees is one in which a large sheet comes down from heaven and is filled with animals that were on the "do not ever eat" list of Peter's upbringing. Peter has adhered to this list since birth, which is why he refuses God's invitation to eat when he says, "By no means, Lord; for I have never eaten anything that is common or unclean" (Acts 10:14). Three times God tells Peter to kill and eat, repeating it for emphasis. When Jesus repeats himself in the Gospels by saying in several places, "Truly, truly," it is his way of saying, "You need to really pay attention here." But when something is repeated three times, it's even more important. For example, in Isaiah 6:3, all the angels declare God to be "holy, holy, holy." This is the only attribute of God repeated consecutively three times in the Bible. When something is stated or occurs three consecutive times, God is really making a point.

God's threefold instruction to Peter to kill and eat nonkosher food rattles Peter to his core. We know this because Luke describes Peter as being "inwardly perplexed" (Acts 10:17). The trajectory of his life has just changed, and it happens with a catalyzing experience of food. By themselves, these kinds of experiences can lack lasting power, but when they work in concert with community and content (which we will talk about later), they become a powerful three-strand cord forming our lives. This is especially true when it comes to ethnic healing and reconciliation.

I have friends who take their university students on annual bus trips for what they call "civil rights tours." Those who attend form a diverse body. On the bus they watch films dealing with the pain of racism and then engage in robust discussions. They sing songs together and read Scripture. They learn what it means to lament and do so after sobering tours of the National Civil Rights Museum and the National Memorial for Peace and Justice. Along the way, they have necessary but painful exchanges. But no one emerges from these trips the same. When combined with community and content, catalyzing experiences tend to get inside of us, leaving us, like Peter, "inwardly perplexed."

My grandfather in the ministry, Dr. John Perkins, speaks autobiographically of his rooftop vision, his Red Sea catalyzing experience. He was viciously beaten by white men in the era of Jim Crow. Bloodied and battered, Dr. Perkins began to feel the levees of hate loosen in his soul. It was there he had to make a decision, and he chose the way of love and forgiveness. This catalyzing experience changed the trajectory of his life, catapulting him to the front lines of the civil rights movement. Today, in the winter years of his life, he has left a legacy of love and hope and healing, all because of that catalyzing experience.

In his book *Bonhoeffer's Black Jesus*, Reggie Williams tells of the time Bonhoeffer took a trip to the Jim Crow South with his African American friend.[3] What he witnessed left Bonhoeffer inwardly perplexed, for here he encountered face to face the ugly injustices exacted on people of color. This experience both sobered and emboldened a young Bonhoeffer, outfitting him with the requisite courage to go back and stand against the atrocities of the Nazi regime. What both changed the trajectory of Bonhoeffer's life and cemented his legacy was the catalyzing experience of this trip to the South.

---

3. Reggie L. Williams, *Bonhoeffer's Black Jesus: Harlem Renaissance Theology and an Ethic of Resistance* (Waco, TX: Baylor University Press, 2014).

CONTENT

Finally, there is the element of content. What this text points to is the most potent kind of content, the very words of God. What forms Peter indelibly is that this experience is rooted in the words of God. God speaks to him on this rooftop. He is not merely hearing the words of a motivational speaker or reading a *New York Times* bestseller, but is listening to the living, active word of God. And when Peter arrives at the "unclean home" of Cornelius where an audience of gentiles awaits him, he declares to them the content, the very word of God, that will likewise transform them in the very way the word had transformed him.

Preachers in the evangelical tradition can make the assumption that if we faithfully mine the Scriptures and unveil to our hearers its message, they will receive it. This is where expository preaching becomes our friend, for it is built on the assumption that we are not speaking our word but God's word. When preachers make their way through books of the Bible, we get out of the way and place our audience in the direct line of sight of the all-powerful, still-speaking God. When we do this, we can rightly claim the promise of Scripture that God's word will not return void (Isaiah 55:11).

This is everything when we talk about matters of race. As you know, our adversary has sought to make race a political or merely sociological issue. But when the preacher comes to texts such as ours and carefully excavates the ancient narrative in such a way as to show the congregation that the agenda is not being driven by CNN, Fox News, or MSNBC, but by the heart and mouth of a holy God, we now position them to deal with God. This truth should give us both courage and great sleep at night. Expository preaching—letting the text set the agenda for the message—is the preacher's best friend, especially when dealing with inflammatory topics such as racism.

CONCLUSION

Community, catalyzing experiences, and content are all found in the gospel of Jesus Christ. The gospel is all about relationships, community, connecting fallen people with a risen Christ and also with one another across ethnic, gender, and class lines (Galatians 3:28). The gospel is also the most significant catalyzing experience one could ever have, for it takes us from death to life. And the gospel extends to us a whole new operating system of how to live and relate to others, which is laid out in much of the New Testament.

But Acts 10 also comes with a warning label, found right on the heels of Luke's narrative in Acts 11: "So when Peter went up to Jerusalem, the circumcision party criticized him" (Acts 11:2). No matter how obviously, carefully, and lovingly we may preach about race, we can expect critique. The pulpit is no place to work out one's self-esteem issues or longings for acceptance. Just about every time I've talked about race over the years, I've had people walk out and send me not-so-nice emails. Many times there is a nugget of truth to their concerns. I could have said things better. But there are plenty of times when I have to rest in a loving God and trust his word to come to fruition.

African theologian and bishop Augustine once wrote, "I must confess that, personally, I have learned many things I never knew before ... just by writing."⁴ Oh, the humility in these words. Augustine is confiding that his writing did not come from being settled on matters before he picked up his pen —no. The very process of writing was redemptively revelatory to him. We might very well exchange "writing" for "preaching." I'm not convinced that, had Peter rejected Christ's

---

4. Peter Brown, *Augustine of Hippo* (Berkeley: University of California Press, 2000), 273.

invitation to follow him and instead chosen to stay on as a fisherman, he would have ever dealt with the prejudices of his heart. It was only through apprenticeship to Christ and his call to preach that God dealt with his prejudice.

Yes, we preachers should use our syntax and training, but by no means does this make us experts in the Scriptures by way of practice. Nor should we allow our lack of life experiences in any area to keep us from proclaiming the whole counsel of God. In fact, it is along the way where we, too, will find ourselves confronted and ultimately changed to look more like Jesus, just like the preacher Peter in our text.

Engaging Communities with the Reconciling Power of the Gospel

Romans 15:7

If you want to mobilize your church family to take practical steps toward racial harmony in your community, I am so excited for you. Our communities are desperate for an answer to the issues that divide us. As you begin, I want to encourage you to start with identity. Activity flows from identity. And if our identity isn't clearly rooted in the person and work of Christ, then our activities won't bear lasting fruit. In this chapter, I'm going to get into some practical principles to guide toward action, but please don't gloss over the time it will take to ensure that your members know that identity comes first. We do not move toward racial reconciliation in order to earn God's love. We move toward racial reconciliation *because* of God's love.

I believe the theme of racial reconciliation is so present throughout all of the Bible that you can choose from many different texts to find encouragement, challenges, and truths to share. One of my favorite places to go to teach our members about reconciliation is the book of Romans. Now, if you are like most typical evangelical Christians, you might be a little surprised by this. Romans might be most known for being packed with theology, but it contains many important principles to help us lead reconciliation in the church.

Often when we teach passages from the book of Romans, we pull out verses and treat them as if they were chapters in a systematic theology book. But that's not how Paul wrote it—so that's not how we should read it. Paul wrote this as a *letter* to a specific people addressing specific issues. If we pull the verses out of that context, they lose some of their intended message. So before we jump into a specific text, let's take some time to look at the historical context for the book.

HISTORICAL CONTEXT

During the time Romans was written, Christianity was spreading, and the way it typically spread was through the Jewish synagogues. If you look throughout Acts, you see how Paul goes to the Jewish synagogues first and then takes the gospel other places (Acts 13:5, 13–14; 17:1–3, 16–17). Since Christianity flowed out of the Jewish faith, it is likely that in most places the Jewish Christians were the leaders of the new church, and Rome would have been no different. But in AD 49, Emperor Claudius banned all Jews from Rome—including Jewish Christians.

Here you had a Jewish/gentile church with Jewish leaders—but then the Jews were expelled. So the gentile Christians were there alone, and they naturally became the leaders of the church. And because they were gentiles, they were not continuing any of the traditional Jewish cultural rituals. When Nero became emperor five years later, the ban was lifted, and the Jewish Christians came back. When they returned, some Jewish Christians must have wondered, "What did you do to our faith! You're not practicing the traditions—you're living like heathens!"[1] The divisions among Roman Christians were entirely exposed. Could they worship together? Could the Jewish Christians serve under the leadership of the gentile Christians? Could the gentiles respect the cultural traditions of the Jews, or would they belittle them for being "weaker" in their faith?

When Paul wrote to the Romans, he hadn't visited Rome yet. Almost every other epistle he wrote was to a people or a place that he had visited, but there are three reasons he wrote to the Romans before going there. The first is that Paul was trying to get to Spain (Romans 15:23–24). He was on a mission to take the gospel there, and he wanted the Roman Christians to send people and financial support with him. But he knew he was going to be delayed in going because he had to first take a gift to the persecuted Christians in Jerusalem (Romans 15:28). Because of this delay, he was concerned that the Judaizers, who had been teaching a different gospel, would get to the Roman church first and that false teachers might infiltrate their people (Romans 3:8; 16:17–18).

The Judaizers preached that the gospel is Christ *plus*: "Christ plus circumcision. Christ plus what you wear. Christ plus traditions. Yes, believe the gospel—but also do certain things." Paul knew that the Judaizers might get to Rome before him, since he was going to Jerusalem first, so he wanted to write to the Romans to preempt the false teaching they were going to encounter.[2]

I believe the third reason for writing is the most prominent, as it also undergirds the other reasons. Paul was writing to

---

1. Randy Colver, *Romans and Reconciliation: The Message of Romans for the Trenches* (Lulu, 2006), 5.

2. Colver, *Romans and Reconciliation*, 17.

address the divisions between Jew and gentile in the church.[3] Paul was a Jew who was also a Roman citizen. His mission, his calling, was to take the gospel to the gentiles. Because of all of these things, Paul was intimately aware of the cultural clashes taking place.

So when he sat down to write the book of Romans, he wasn't just deciding to write down a whole bunch of doctrinal truths. No, he was writing to real Christians facing deadly divisions that could compromise his mission to Spain and compromise the integrity of a faith-based gospel being preached in the churches. Throughout the book, sometimes it seems like Paul is speaking to the gentiles. Other times, it feels like he's talking to the Jewish Christians. And that's because he is! He is going back and forth between the two groups, addressing each side, working to bring racial reconciliation through the gospel.

THEOLOGICAL THEMES

Now that we have a baseline understanding of the historical backdrop for the book of Romans, it's easier to identify the theological themes throughout the book. The two theological pillars in the book of Romans are righteousness and reconciliation. The theme of righteousness speaks to the question, How does Christ restore our relationship with God? And the theme of reconciliation speaks to the question, How does Christ restore our relationship with our brothers and sisters? Here is where understanding the historical background is so critical. Check out this excerpt from the book *The New Testament Speaks*:

> The context in which Paul introduces the concept of the righteousness of God is the most striking feature of his

---

3. Colver, *Romans and Reconciliation*, 17.

exposition. Every passage in which Paul speaks of righteousness occurs within a larger context discussing the relationship of Jews and Gentiles in the one church of Christ. In each instance they illustrate the thoroughly missionary character of Romans. Paul's teaching on justification by faith is best understood as the answer to a persistent question: How is it possible for the Jew and the Gentile to stand on the same level of advantage before God?[4]

Righteousness with God leads to reconciled relationships with our brothers and sisters. Throughout the book, Paul emphasizes the idea that we all come to Christ on an equal basis. Why? Because he was answering the questions the Jewish Christians were struggling with. Compare that to how we often use Romans today. Many of us use Romans to pull out verses as prooftexts for our theological camps. We use the truths of the letter as weapons to divide the church—which is the very opposite of what the book was intended for! Romans was not written to increase our head knowledge. It was written to give us instructions for living out our identity as reconcilers, to show us how our righteousness transforms all of our earthly relationships.

Throughout Romans, you see a lot of calls to obedience. When Paul talks about obedience, he's not simply talking about keeping a moral code; he's talking about how you are treating your neighbor—he's talking about reconciliation. Obedience in Romans *is* reconciliation. Yes, the moral issues are there, and

---

4. G. W. Baker, W. L. Lane, and J. R. Michaels, *The New Testament Speaks* (New York: HarperCollins, 1969), 192, cited in D. Madvig, "The Missionary Preaching of Paul: A Problem in New Testament Theology," *Journal of the Evangelical Theological Society* 20.2 (1977): 150.

obedience does involve honoring the morals God outlines in Scripture. But sin has never been *just* about keeping or breaking moral rules. Sin is a violation of relationship. Sin broke our relationship with God. It brought division between man and woman. Paul is telling us that the gospel is the answer for that. The gospel is the reconciling power to bring healing to our relationship with God and our relationships with one another.

DEEP DIVE

At this point, we would be able to look at just about any passage in Romans with a more holistic understanding of Paul's intended message. But let's take a quick look at Romans 15:7. Now remember—Paul is addressing Jew and gentile Christians who are divided. They are not worshiping together. They are not unified as one body of Christ. They have divided along lines of race and ethnicity. So he writes, "Therefore welcome one another as Christ has welcomed you, for the glory of God." The CSB uses the word "accept" in place of "welcome." The driving principle here is one of hospitality. "Accept" and "welcome" are both words that imply love and kindness and unity. But I think the key phrase to understanding Paul's meaning is "as Christ has welcomed you." How did Christ welcome us? His welcome certainly wasn't a passive, "come if you want to" kind of welcome. His welcome was an active pursuit of us, full of intentional sacrifice in order to bridge the divide between us. The way Christ has welcomed us is the way of the cross. He laid down his life so that we could be unified with him. And that is the way we are to welcome one another. We are to be a people who are willing to lay down our lives, our cultural preferences, and our preconceived notions of other people. We are to be a people who do not sit passively by in the face of division but are willing to sacrifice everything we have to see reconciliation take place.

If we are a people who welcome one another like this, then the world might truly know that we belong to Jesus because of our love. And if we learn to accept one another as Christ has accepted us, then and only then will we have something to offer our communities. As local churches, we cannot give what we do not have. If we do not have unity within the body, then we cannot offer it to our neighbors. So begin within. And as you work on internal unity and begin to offer that hospitality to your neighbors, I want you to consider the "person of peace" principle.

This idea is common in a lot of evangelism, missionary, or church-planting strategies. As you go into a new place, you look for a person who can connect you into the community: someone who is kind to you, who is willing to build a relationship with you, and who ultimately will be your guide into becoming part of the community. When used well, this strategy can be effective in helping us reach communities in culturally meaningful ways. However, the strategy falls short if we end there. The work is not done once we find a person of peace. We need to go one step further and work to *become* the person of peace—because that is the way Christ welcomed us. He became our peace.

My wife has done an incredible job of this in our neighborhood. She has spent hours investing in relationships and systemic change in our local elementary school. Countless children and parents in our neighborhood know her, trust her, and call her when there is a need. When a new person wants to get connected to our neighborhood—Angie is the person to do it. She is constantly doing the work of bridging divides, overcoming barriers, and fighting for unity in our neighborhood. When we first moved into the neighborhood, it wasn't like this. Angie had to find people of peace who would let her in and show her the ropes. Now, she has become one of the people of peace for our neighborhood.

APPLICATION

You may be already familiar with the *3 Circles: Life Conversation Guide*.[5] It's a wonderful tool used to share the gospel. In our church, we often use it as a tool to help us learn how to apply the gospel to our everyday lives and increase our fluency in the gospel. Colossians 2:6 says, "Therefore, as you received Christ Jesus the Lord, so walk in him." The same gospel that gives us eternal life is the gospel that infuses life into our everyday lives. Let me show you how the three circles can help give practical application from this text in Romans to your context.

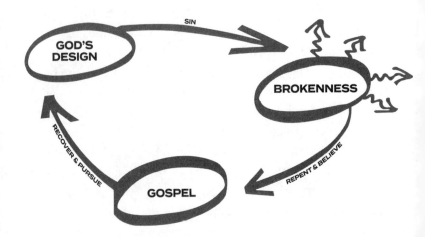

---

5. "3 Circles: Life Conversation Guide," Life on Mission (accessed October 11, 2020), http://lifeonmissionbook.com/conversation-guide.

In Romans, we see brokenness displayed in the division of the church. They were not meeting together. They were not treating one another with love or kindness. Once we identify the brokenness, we go back and ask the question, What was God's original design for this? God's design is for his people to be unified in Christ (John 17:21) and for there to be no divisions within the body of Christ (Galatians 3:28). God's design is for his people to be known for their love (John 13:35). God's design is for his people to support one another—even when some of our convictions differ (Romans 14:1–23). But the sins of ethnocentrism and superiority infiltrated the Roman Christians and pulled them away from God's design. That sin led them to the brokenness of division in the church. The only way back to God's design is through the gospel. The Roman Christians needed to repent from their sin. Paul called out those who were living in blatant sin; he called out those who said they didn't sin but did; he called out the self-righteous and told them that there was none righteous. All have sinned. They all had to repent and believe in the gospel. Then, and only then, would they be able to recover and pursue God's original design.

And how would they recover and pursue God's original design? Through hospitality. By presenting their bodies as living sacrifices and welcoming one another as Christ had welcomed them (Romans 15:7).

At the end of the day, Paul is saying that if we are not reconciled, there's somewhere we are not believing the gospel. Think of it this way: On a Sunday morning, when everyone walks into a church building, they walk in with faith that the building isn't going to collapse. If you say, "I have faith but I'm not going in," would anyone believe your faith was genuine? No way—because faith produces something. In the same way, Christ has given us the ministry of reconciliation. We are new creations.

Our faith in Christ leads to a transformed identity, and as new creations we live as reconcilers.

CONCLUSION

Finally, as you are mobilizing your people to become the people of peace in your communities, here are some practical principles to keep in mind. You may be looking for a step-by-step guide, but every context is different, and no one strategy works in each place. These principles will enable you to adapt the reconciling message of Romans to your context.

- Constantly work on internal reconciliation and unity. You cannot give what you do not have.

- Do not place cultural identities and preferences above unity in Christ. Fight against cultural relativism. Do not excuse sin and blame it on culture. Fight to align every person and decision with the gospel.

- Do not belittle or ignore cultural identities and differences. Don't pretend like they don't exist. Instead, honor cultural nuances and differences, and celebrate the beauty they bring.

- Go from finding people of peace in your community to becoming people of peace in your community.

- Look for issues that affect the whole community—things that everyone has something at stake in. For example, in our neighborhood the gentrified community cares about school performance because it impacts their property values, and the indigenous community cares because their kids are in the school. Working to bring excellence and overcome systemic brokenness in our local schools is something we can unify our neighborhood around.

- Remember that Jesus is the answer—not you.

- Don't copy and paste what you've seen done in other places. Work to identify a contextualized answer to the divisions you are facing.

- Don't reinvent the wheel. Learn from others and apply those principles in a way that works for your church family and community.

I pray that, as you work to mobilize your members to engage your community with the reconciling power of the gospel through the person and work of Jesus, your church would grow in unity. I pray that God would give you wisdom to lead toward contextualized answers to the needs of your church family and your neighbors. I pray that you would be a people known for your love.

Giving Greater Honor to the "Minority" in Your Midst

1 Corinthians 12:12–26

As a second-generation Korean American, I straddle the line between the East and the West. In my upbringing, I was told to be "American" (a euphemism for white) in public and "Korean" at home and at our first-generation Korean church. I hold within me the values of Western individualism and Eastern collectivism. Within me resides both the American spirit of independence and the Korean spirit of filial piety. For better or worse, these forces shape how I live in this world God created.

Our understanding of honor is heavily influenced by our culture. As a Korean American, I view honor through both a Western and an Eastern lens. My Western sensibilities tell me that honor primarily goes to the one who earns it. It is given to the ones who deserve it through their merits. My Eastern sensibilities, however, tell me that honor primarily goes to those who came before me, regardless of their merits. This is because relationships weigh more than achievement (though achievement brings honor to the relationship). In my opinion, there is gold and dross in both of these views. It is appropriate to give honor to those who have achieved and accomplished much—especially if it came at a great sacrifice and led to much fruitfulness.

81

But this can turn into a form of dehumanization that leads to looking down on those who don't produce what society values. It is also appropriate to give honor to those through whom God has brought you forth. But this can turn into a form of idolatry that leads us to follow our family above following God. The first approach gives honor based on production. The second gives honor as a result of progeny.

Now, neither of these views necessarily contradicts the Bible, but the practice of them can certainly go awry. Further, the Scriptures suggest another form of giving honor that is pertinent (and arguably, more gospel centered) to the issues surrounding racial and ethnic division and unity. Together, we will explore a third way of giving honor that can serve as a helpful framework that also rounds the edges of both of these approaches.

HONOR IN THE CORINTHIAN CHURCH

The Scriptures use the Greek word *timē* (*ti-may*) to describe what we know as honor. The word *timē* generally means "worth," "evaluation," "honor," or "price." In certain contexts, *timē* can convey more specific meanings that include notions of "appraisal," "assessment," "dignity," or "honorarium." To "give *timē*," then, using the verb form *timaō* (*ti-mah-oh*), is to properly value and esteem something. To "give *timē*" is to adorn so as to give special attention to something or someone.

In 1 Corinthians 12:23–24, as Paul addresses the divisions within the church of Corinth, he asserts that the remedy to such divisions is found in giving honor to those who have been deprived of it. It is the way in which Paul calls the Corinthian church to care for what we would understand as the minorities in its midst. And as we see throughout Scripture, we honor others (especially those who are marginalized) because Christ honored us.

To be a minority is to be without adequate power. The term "minority" is often misunderstood to refer to numerical realities, but within the social sciences, a minority is not primarily defined by numbers. Instead, minorities are those who lack social standing (this is why black people in South Africa are considered a minority, even though they are the numerical majority). It refers to people groups that hold little to no significant positions of social power in a given society based on how that society defines a person's worth. This dynamic is essentially what we see in Paul's first letter to the Corinthians.

This letter was written to a church situated in a proud and booming Roman city. It was a city known for its vibrant commerce along strategic trade routes, which connected the East and the West. In the twenty-first century, Corinth could be compared to Singapore or Hong Kong, which are international gateway cities. It was a cosmopolitan city where old and new religions bustled alongside one another. It was also a diverse city full of new money and opportunities, made up of free Romans, native Greeks, and immigrants from near and far.

The church in Corinth was not immune to the influences of the culture around it. Paul writes about how the "spirit of the world" (2:12) or the "wisdom of the world" (1:20; 3:19) bled into the church. In many ways, the Corinthian church mimicked the patterns of the broader society. The Corinthian society was stratified between the haves and the have-nots, and this same stratification entered into the church (11:22). In the ways the broader society was divided, so was the church.

In 1 Corinthians 11:17–34, Paul addresses the divisions and factions that had emerged in the church. These divisions were pronounced during the Lord's Supper. Those who had means got drunk in excess, while those who did not have means went hungry and were shamed and humiliated (vv. 20–22). Basically, those who were privileged in society neglected the needs of those who didn't possess such privileges, and instead of using their privilege to benefit others, they used it to maintain their own status. Paul reminds them that this is not the way it is supposed to be.

Then, in 12:1–11, Paul addresses the arbitrary and ungodly stratification that emerged along the lines of spiritual gifts (where some gifts were perceived to be superior to others), reminding the Corinthians that God gives gifts to people in distinct ways by the power of the Holy Spirit. Spiritual gifts are not things we have rights to, but things we have responsibility for. As such, we are required to use them for the glory of God and the good of our neighbor. Paul heard that a pecking order had developed based on spiritual gifts. Those who had certain gifts marked as more significant moved up in status, while those who had other gifts dropped down. Some were elevated, while others were lowered. As a result, people were sorted into superior and inferior groups. In light of this, in 12:12–26, Paul defends the essential diversity of the body (vv. 12–14), elevates those who are lowly (vv. 15–20), and humbles the proud (vv. 16–26). Paul makes it clear that God designed the church to be unified in diversity, not in uniformity, and that every member of the body is essential to the functioning and the flourishing of the whole body.

In 12:12–13, Paul writes, "For just as the body is one and has many members, and all the members of the body, though many, are one body, so it is with Christ. For in one Spirit we were all baptized into one body—Jews or Greeks, slaves or free—and all were made to drink of one Spirit." Though Paul could have limited the divisions he identified to spiritual gifts, he deliberately highlights that Jews and Greeks, slaves and free, were all baptized into one body, knowing that these were well-known lines that fractured the church and the broader society. The ancient world was divided along lines of ethnicity/race (Jews and gentiles) and class (slave and free), as the world is today, so Paul reminds the Corinthians that the things that had divided them in their former lives no longer should in their new lives as Christians.

Although the world was divided along the lines of what we would today consider ethnicity/race and class, those who followed Christ were stitched together by the Holy Spirit regardless of their background. Over and over, Paul reminds believers that the church ought to demonstrate the power of the gospel through its unified diversity. The way he calls the Corinthian church to do this is by "giving greater honor" to the parts that they consider less honorable or valuable. Here, he appeals to the ways they instinctively know to do this as they pay special attention to the more vulnerable parts of their bodies (this is what Paul is alluding to in 12:23–24).

GIVING GREATER HONOR TODAY

This has significant implications for how we navigate the divisions that have infiltrated our churches from the broader society. It doesn't matter whether your local congregation is diverse or not—we live in a diverse country full of diverse people, and if we do not educate, train, and disciple our congregants to understand the diverse world they live in, they will carry narrow and harmful perspectives into the world where they represent Christ. But what does it mean to give greater honor along the societally fractured lines that have infected the church (such as race), or the ones that have emerged from within the church (such as spiritual gifts)?

One way is to preach the gospel into the issues that emerge along racial lines (perhaps this is why you picked up this book, and my hope is that this section both encourages you in this as well as equips you to serve your people in it). As I travel and speak throughout the country, one of the most common series of questions I get from Christians of color within predominantly white evangelical churches and institutions is, Will you actually speak up on issues that matter to us? And if you do, will you speak in a way that will help our brothers and sisters in Christ see the urgency to live into the call of God's kingdom? Or will you water things down and soften the message out of self-preservation and promotion, perpetuating the racial status quo that makes it difficult for us to dwell together with our fellow siblings in Christ? These questions are hard, but real.

We are often tempted to believe that silence and neutrality are virtuous stances to take on these issues. After all, Proverbs 17:28 tells us, "Even a fool who keeps silent is considered wise; when he closes his lips, he is deemed intelligent." But in matters of righteousness and justice, we must not conflate silence and neutrality with wisdom. Far too often, those who remain silent in the face of injustice benefit from the unjust status quo. The Rev. Dr. Martin Luther King Jr. once wrote, "We will remember not the words of our enemies, but the silence of our friends."[1] He also wrote, "The greatest tragedy of this period of social transition was not the strident clamor of the bad people, but the appalling silence of the good people." This is a sentiment shared by those in the margins of any community or society throughout the generations. In his reflections on the Holocaust, Elie

---

1. "Martin Luther King Jr. Quotes: In His Own Words," *Birmingham Times*, January 15, 2018, https://www.birminghamtimes.com/2018/01/some-of-dr-martin-luther-king-jr-s-profound-quotes.

Wiesel wrote, "I swore never to be silent whenever and wherever humans endure suffering and humiliation. We must always take sides. Neutrality helps the oppressor, never the victim. Silence encourages the tormenter, never the tormented."[2]

We cannot reach wholeness unless we are willing to address the brokenness. You can't heal the racial wounds you refuse to treat. And unless we are able to address the brokenness in its fullness, we will only get to partial healing. As Soong-Chan Rah writes in his book *Prophetic Lament*,

> The depth of pain endemic to racial hostility requires full disclosure for complete healing. The church should become the place where the fullness of suffering is expressed in a safe environment. Liturgy, worship, leadership, small groups and other aspects of church life should provide the safe place where the fullness of suffering can be set free. Stories of suffering can never be buried when lament is an important and central aspect of the church's worship life.[3]

PREACHING THE WHOLE GOSPEL

However, in many evangelical churches, those who are racialized as white often see racial problems in one way, and racial minorities often see the exact same thing in another way, which makes it difficult to come to a consensus on how to address the racial divides. Often, the perspectives and experiences of Christians of color are denied, dismissed, and discounted because they are not the perspectives and experiences of the

---

2. Elie Wiesel, *Night*, trans. Marion Wiesel (New York: Hill and Wang, 2006), 118.

3. Soong-Chan Rah, *Prophetic Lament: A Call to Justice in Troubled Times* (Downers Grove, IL: InterVarsity Press, 2015), 58.

dominant white majority. As such, many Christians of color find it difficult to shine a light on the things they feel like others don't want illuminated. But I wonder what it would be like if we took the time to truly understand what it is like to walk in the shoes of someone who comes from a different background from us, to try to see things as they see them, and to take their perspective as fellow siblings in Christ—starting from a place that they might know their own experience better than we do. Perhaps this is another way to "give greater honor."

This is not to say that we ought to force a discussion of this issue into a biblical passage that has nothing to do with it. We should certainly avoid eisegesis. However, more passages relate to issues of ethnicity and race than we might realize. In the New Testament alone, the books of Luke, Acts, Romans, 1 Corinthians, Ephesians, Galatians, Colossians, and Revelation explicitly address matters of ethnicity/race that would challenge the status quo of twenty-first century evangelicalism. If you simply preach through the Bible faithfully, it is impossible to ignore the numerous ways in which the Bible speaks directly or indirectly into issues of ethnicity and race. Unfortunately, the ways that people have been misdiscipled and miseducated on the topic of race have led many preachers to miss what is plainly there. Racialization has created what philosopher John Rawls might call "a veil of ignorance" around how race actually functions in our society and in our churches.

This is also not to say that we do not employ wisdom when preaching on such issues. We ought to be wise in our approach. But I have found that when it comes to applying the gospel to contentious issues (especially issues that have become unnecessarily politicized), we often confuse fear with wisdom. God calls us to be courageous where the Scriptures are courageous. We need not be afraid to go where God has already gone. As historian Jemar Tisby writes in his book *The Color of Compromise*, "We have the power, through God, to leave behind the compromised Christianity that makes its peace with racism and to live out Christ's call to a courageous faith."[4] Unfortunately, we often allow fear to drive us more than faith on issues of racial justice. This is why Christians of color often express frustration and lament around silence by white Christians on issues surrounding justice. They often express a desire for their white brothers and sisters in Christ to speak on issues of social justice with the same conviction as they do on issues surrounding religious freedom and the sanctity of life.

In fact, Christians of color often express a desire for the scope of sanctity of life issues to extend from the womb all the way to the tomb. Shortly after the 2019 Dove Awards aired, Christian music artist Kirk Franklin boycotted any events affiliated with the Dove Awards, Gospel Music Association, or Trinity Broadcasting Network because his acceptance speeches were edited in both 2016 and 2019 to exclude portions where he addressed the senseless deaths of innocent black men and women (e.g., Philando Castile, Walter Scott, and Atatiana Jefferson) at the hands of white police officers (as well as the deaths of five white police officers at the hands of a black gunman in Dallas). He stated, "As Christians, when we say nothing, we're saying something." He then declared, "Not only did they edit my speech, they edited the African American experience."[5] This is just one instance that demonstrates how

---

4. Jemar Tisby, *The Color of Compromise: The Truth about the American Church's Complicity in Racism* (Grand Rapids: Zondervan, 2019), 215.

5. Sarah Pulliam Bailey, "Kirk Franklin Boycotts Gospel Awards Show after Comments on Black Violence Edited on TV," *Washington Post*, October 28, 2019, https://www.washingtonpost.com/religion/2019/10/28/kirk-franklin-boycotts-awards-show-after-comments-black-violence-edited-by-tbn.

the Christian worldview ought to be consistently for life, in and beyond the womb.

In 2020, in the midst of the COVID-19 pandemic, the world erupted over the deaths of George Floyd and Breonna Taylor at the hands of those who swore to protect and serve them, in addition to the vigilante lynching of Ahmaud Arbery earlier in the year. Many also spoke up against the rise of overt anti-Asian racism that emerged throughout the nation as the novel coronavirus was associated with Asians and Asian Americans. In the midst of the racial strife, many white evangelical Christians spoke up in ways that Christians of color had not seen before. And while many Christians of color were encouraged, there were also many who wondered why white Christians had stayed silent for so long until it cost nearly nothing to finally speak up and do something. The words Russell Moore once said are worth considering: "The temptation that evangelical Christianity always has is to be as authoritative and as prophetic as the people with money in the room will allow us to be."[6]

Theologian and founding editor of *Christianity Today* Carl F. H. Henry once wrote, "If the church fails to apply the central truth of Christianity to social problems correctly, someone else will do so incorrectly."[7] It is worth asking whether we are in the polarized state we are in because we have failed to apply the gospel to the social problems we see. Surveying the evangelical landscape, Henry wrote, "Social justice is not simply an appendage to the evangelistic message; it is an intrinsic part of the whole, without which the preaching of the gospel

---

6. Russell Moore, CCCU gathering, Washington DC, January 30, 2019.

7. Carl F. H. Henry, *Aspects of Christian Social Ethics* (Grand Rapids: Eerdmans, 1964), 82.

is truncated. Theology devoid of social justice is a deforming weakness of much present-day evangelical witness."[8] This was written in the late 1970s.

Preachers are entrusted with the discipleship of our congregations from the pulpit, and a real aspect of discipleship is teaching people what it looks like to recontextualize and apply the gospel message to every facet of life in this world. According to Fuller Seminary President Mark Labberton, "When preaching plays to the culture without substantially critiquing and engaging it, it becomes part of the problem. Sermons that only apply to the individual and to the inner life of the disciple without raising biblical questions about our public lives are also a factor."[9] Essentially, we are to preach Christ into every area, but in order to do so, we must venture into the areas we are preaching Christ. Preaching is speaking the truth of God into the world that God made, and a critical element of that is applying God's truth into every facet of the world in which we live. This is why Kathy Khang writes, "The challenge to raise your voice is about doing the good work of the good news. It's about calling forth others: an invocation for all and a provocation to some. Our lives should affect the world around us if we are bearers of God's image as well as an embodiment of good news."[10]

If we desire to be the body of Christ as God intended, we must be willing to recontextualize and apply the gospel to the issues that affect those members who have been deemed less valuable according to the eyes of the world. May we not be

---

8. Carl F. H. Henry, "Good News for the Oppressed," in *God, Revelation, and Authority: The God Who Speaks and Shows* (Wheaton, IL: Crossway, 1979), 4:551.

9. Mark Labberton, *The Dangerous Act of Worship: Living God's Call to Justice* (Downers Grove, IL: InterVarsity Press, 2007).

10. Kathy Khang, *Raise Your Voice: Why We Stay Silent and How to Speak Up* (Downers Grove, IL: InterVarsity Press, 2019).

like the Corinthian church, whose problem was that, as New Testament scholar Gordon Fee writes, "Although they were the Christian church in Corinth, an inordinate amount of Corinth was yet in them."[11] If there are divisions in the church that mirror the divisions of the rest of society, perhaps we should take some time to search the Scriptures, listen to the members of our church who come from groups that are often deemed less honorable, explore academic research on the matters facing us, and boldly proclaim the gospel into everything that Christ lays claim to. May we remember Paul's words in 1 Corinthians 12:26: "If one member suffers, all suffer together; *if one member is honored, all rejoice together.*"

---

11. Gordon D. Fee, *The First Epistle to the Corinthians*, New International Commentary on the New Testament (Grand Rapids: Eerdmans, 1987), 4.

9 | Ray Ortlund

The Ministry of Reconciliation

2 Corinthians 5:18

Every generation of God's people is tested in particular ways. Our churches in America today are under tremendous pressure at two flashpoints of intense controversy: sexual integrity and racial reconciliation. If we remain faithful to Christ at all other points but cave on these two issues, we will betray him precisely where his call rings most clearly in our time. A wise voice has articulated it this way:

> If I profess with the loudest voice and clearest exposition every portion of the truth of God except precisely that little point which the world and the devil are at the moment attacking, I am not confessing Christ, however boldly I may be professing Christ. Where the battle rages, there the loyalty of the soldier is proved. And to be steady on all the battle fields besides is merely flight and disgrace, if he flinches at that point.[1]

---

1. This comes from a historical novel set during the Reformation by Elizabeth Rundle Charles, *The Chronicles of the Schönberg Cotta Family* (New York: M. W. Dodd, 1864), 321.

As we stand before the Lord, let us accept—deeply accept, bravely and cheerfully—what faithfulness to him requires of us and our churches in this generation.

One difference between these two burning issues—sexual integrity and racial reconciliation—is that our culture is against us on sexual ethics but, for the most part, with us on racial harmony. So, as we bear witness before our Lord and before our world, we really have no excuse for failing to demonstrate the beauty of racial reconciliation.

I want to do two things in this chapter. One, I want to prove from Scripture the authority of our ministry of reconciliation. Two, I want to propose some categories for follow-through, so that we might—imperfectly but visibly—demonstrate our ministry of reconciliation in ways our world can see. This chapter is a statement of personal conviction. Much more should be said. But I hope this modest contribution will stir us all "to love and good works" (Hebrews 10:24).

THE AUTHORITY OF
OUR MINISTRY

The Bible tells us that "God ... gave us the ministry of reconciliation" (2 Corinthians 5:18). That ministry pursues reconciliation at two levels. First, it leads sinners into peace with God vertically: "Be reconciled to God" (2 Corinthians 5:20). Second, it leads those sinners into peace with one another horizontally: "Make room in your hearts for us" (2 Corinthians 7:2). How could it be otherwise? The ministry of *reconciliation* overcomes limits to its relevance and reach.

But let's notice what 2 Corinthians 5:18 does *not* say: "God gives us moments of reconciliation now and then, when it suits our purposes." No, *God* gave us the *ministry* of *reconciliation*.

If God gave it, then it isn't optional but authoritative. If it is our ministry, then it isn't a preference, but it's all we do and how we roll. And if it's about reconciliation, then we rejoice to deconstruct the lines of angry aloofness that we sinners have created by our pride. God, with all of his authority, gave us the ministry, with all of its urgency, of reconciliation, with all of its courage.

We know, moreover, that the New Testament calls us to pursue our ministry of reconciliation across racial lines. The Bible tells us that Christ himself is our peace, "who has made us both one and has broken down in his flesh the dividing wall of hostility" (Ephesians 2:14). Again, let's notice what Ephesians 2:14 does *not* say: "He has made us both the same." The gospel is not like a blender, whipping the ingredients together into a mushy blur. Coming into Christ by faith alone, we remain who we are, and we become God's racially and culturally diverse new creation, the body of Christ. Here is something else Ephesians 2:14 does *not* say: "He has made us both equal." The gospel does not allow for "separate but equal" racial hypocrisy hiding beneath an empty slogan. The gospel is bold: Christ has made us *one*. We remain diverse, but we become inseparable.

If, therefore, God has given us the ministry of reconciliation, and if Christ died to make us all one, then our churches must stand out as obvious demonstrations of unity across the lines of worldly politics, culture wars, and selfish resentments. We can prevail, by Spirit-given humility and courage, over the whole bloodstained history of American racial wickedness. But we cannot be subtle about this. We must be as obvious as the authority of God and the cross of Christ call for. Let's dare to take new steps.

THE DEMONSTRATION
OF OUR MINISTRY

In 1974, I heard Francis Schaeffer preach at the Lausanne Congress on World Evangelization. His unforgettable sermon gave me new categories for courageous ministry in hard times. After hearing Schaeffer, I knew what to reach for.

Schaeffer asked the question, "What is the Christian's task in the world today?" His answer was *not* evangelism. Evangelism can seem canned, he said, like a sales pitch. But when evangelism is pursued as part of a larger reality, as a part of a truly beautiful church, it can be convincing. What, then, does a church look like when it is true to the gospel and to the urgency of our times? Schaeffer proposed two contents, followed by two realities.[2]

The first kind of content in a faithful church is sound doctrine: "clear doctrinal content concerning the central elements of Christianity."[3] This strong biblical message stands in contrast to the weak, pragmatic rolls of the dice churches sometimes settle for.

The second kind of content in a faithful church is honest answers to honest questions: "Christianity demands that we have enough compassion to learn the questions of our generation."[4] If we listen respectfully to others and try to satisfy their doubts and reservations about the gospel, they might listen to us.

But as important as biblical and missional content is, content alone is not enough for our churches to become living

---

2. The text of Schaeffer's remarks to the 1974 Lausanne Congress were reprinted in the book *Two Contents, Two Realities*, available in Francis A. Schaeffer, *The Complete Works of Francis A. Schaeffer: A Christian Worldview*, vol. 3 (Westchester, IL: Crossway Books, 1982).

3. Schaeffer, *Complete Works*, 3:407.

4. Schaeffer, *Complete Works*, 3:414.

proof of the ministry of reconciliation. Schaeffer proposed two realities as well.

The first reality is true spirituality, that is, ongoing personal connection with the living Christ. Schaeffer put it plainly: "There is nothing more ugly in all the world, nothing which more turns people aside, than a dead orthodoxy."[5] Sound doctrine and respectful interactions won't get us far without looking to our Lord for wisdom, love, and strength moment by moment. Apart from him, we can do *nothing* (John 15:5).

The second reality takes us to the heart of our concern in this chapter—the beauty of human relationships. Schaeffer said, "True Christianity produces beauty as well as truth. ... If we do not show beauty in the way we treat each other, then in the eyes of the world and in the eyes of our own children, we are destroying the truth we proclaim."[6] The beauty of human relationships is a common blind spot among us Christians who sincerely but incompletely accept the gospel. Our orthodox doctrinal statements can even make us proud, which makes us *less* convincing. The truth of gospel doctrine must create the beauty of gospel culture in our churches. When we come under the full authority of the ministry of reconciliation, we start demanding of ourselves that we translate our biblical concepts into sacrificial relationships that the world can see as Christlike. Without the *beauty* of our Lord, we are trifling with his truth even as we think we are upholding his truth.

Schaeffer concluded, "When there are the two contents and the two realities, we will begin to see something profound happen in our generation."[7] I agree. And I believe *his four cate-*

---

5. Schaeffer, *Complete Works*, 3:417.
6. Schaeffer, *Complete Works*, 3:417, 419.
7. Schaeffer, *Complete Works*, 3:422.

gories offer a hopeful framework of response for any church today that, for Jesus' sake, longs to speak with prophetic power.

Every one of us can begin somewhere. Every one of us can follow through with some new step, as we are led by the Lord. In his mercy, he can make that step obvious.

ONE SMALL STEP

Our Lord helped me in just this way several years ago. I have many shortcomings in my ministry, but here is one step this white pastor was led to take under the authority of the ministry of reconciliation. We all painfully remember when Dylann Roof, a white supremacist, gunned down nine worshipers at Emanuel African Methodist Episcopal Church in Charleston, South Carolina, in 2015. That week, as I looked to Sunday morning, I knew I had to respond. If I remained silent and proceeded with business as usual on that Sunday, I knew that I would in fact be saying something, and clearly too. I would be clearly denying that God has given Immanuel Church in Nashville the ministry of reconciliation. I would be clearly denying that the death of Christ has made us one. I would be clearly announcing to the world that my priorities were not shaped by the gospel but by something less. So, I could not do nothing. I had to say something. But I wanted yet more—I wanted to make my faith in Christ unmistakably clear, and even visibly obvious.

As I thought it through, I saw one step I could take, small as it was. I went to a T-shirt store in Nashville and had them make for me a special shirt that said in big, bold letters on the front, "SHOOT ME TOO," and on the back, "#Charleston." And I meant it. I wanted Dylann Roof and every white supremacist to know that those black Christians in Charleston and this white pastor in Nashville are *one*. We are reconciled to God and to one another. That miracle of grace overrules my old self and redefines my new self in Christ. I would never want the Dylann Roofs of this world to wonder whether maybe, because I am a white man, I am secretly on their side. I wanted to make it obvious to everyone that I am *one* with the black Christians murdered in Charleston—so much so that if any white supremacist anywhere is going to shoot them, he should come and shoot me too. If he hates them, he should hate me too. If he considers them unworthy to live, he should consider me unworthy to live too. And if some white supremacist actually takes me up on my offer and does shoot me, then, by God's grace, I will thank him for the honor of being identified with the suffering body of Christ.

Charles Haddon Spurgeon, looking back on the early days of his walk with Christ, expressed the mentality of reconciliation:

> I felt that I could not be happy without fellowship with the people of God. I wanted to be wherever they were; and if anybody ridiculed them, I wished to be ridiculed with them; and if people had an ugly name for them, I wanted to be called by that ugly name; for I felt that unless I suffered with Christ in his humiliation, I could not expect to reign with him in his glory.[8]

I felt that way too. So I prepared my words of lament for that Sunday morning. And I wore my T-shirt of solidarity throughout the service. It was such a small thing to do that I am embarrassed to mention it. But my conscience could rest in knowing that I had said and done *something* to take my stand for the ministry of reconciliation. And having taken that one simple step, I was ready for my next step. And so was Immanuel Church.

---

8. C. H. Spurgeon, "The Best Donation," in *The Metropolitan Tabernacle Pulpit Sermons* 37 (London: Passmore & Alabaster, 1891), 629.

What is he calling *you* to do for the ministry of reconciliation? However he leads you, it will cost you something. But when you come to the end, you will know that you stood clearly for Christ in *the* spiritual conflict of your generation. You didn't play it safe, you didn't keep your head down, you didn't wait it out. You took your stand. Well done!

I conclude with a word from another of my spiritual heroes, Anglican Bishop Festo Kivengere of Uganda. However hard our battle might be, let's always remember this:

> The cross is practical. It is God moving in love to meet violent men and women, facing violence and suffering for us. Your faith was born in violence. Your faith was born on Calvary. It can stand anything. It is an all-weather faith. Don't imagine you can only be a Christian when everything is smooth. Christians shine better when everything is just the opposite. Your faith was born in blood and sweat in the loneliness of Calvary. You can stand any test.[9]

---

9. Festo Kivengere, *When God Moves in Revival* (Wheaton, IL: Tyndale House, 1973), 16.

The Gospel and Ethnic Justice

Galatians 2:11–14

Jesus' ministry frequently pressed on issues of ethnic and other cultural divisions, if only because his ministry context was fraught with ethnic and cultural tensions. Indeed, the world has been beset with such things from Genesis 3 onward. Since then, while many people have had a variety of options in navigating or mitigating these tensions, some have had little to no choice at all. Because of the circumstances of life and the systems of the culture, they lack the power or influence to actualize the equality of personhood and dignity bestowed on all by their Creator.

So when Jesus declares in his Beatitudes, for instance, that the poor are blessed and the meek will inherit the earth, he is effectively upending the system of cultural currency. His kingdom is to be a cleansing of the temple of the fallen world, a prophetic judgment against standards of power and preference built on worldly standards such as monetary riches or racial makeup. When Jesus does provocative things such as cursing a fig tree or making a Samaritan the hero of a parable, he is declaring a resetting of the world's standards of righteousness.

The mission of the early church, then, produced a volatile assemblage of cultures. Indeed, making "one new man" out of

Jews and gentiles (Ephesians 2:15) was (and *is*) an inevitable spiritual by-product of gospel proclamation to Jew and gentile alike, without distinction. The gospel brings spiritual order to the demonic chaos masquerading as cultural propriety. When we see the first hint of an ethnic rift in the early church in Acts 6 as the Greek believers accuse the Jewish believers of neglecting Greek widows with the benevolence funds, the church's response is the establishing of the diaconate.

The problem is always there. But so is the solution.

The holy God has made all people equal. We are to show no partiality for any reason, whether social or cultural or ethnic. We are justified by grace alone received through faith alone, and the law cannot help us in that regard except to level the playing field of our universal neediness for salvation in Christ. Showing partiality is a violation of the gospel because we are justified by faith, not works. In the gospel, then, God is not eradicating ethnic distinctions but ethnic preferentialism.

Many objections to the concept of ethnic (or racial) justice today focus on minimizing differences. "The gospel makes us colorblind," or so the arguments go. But this is not just impossible; it's unnecessary. The Lord has created us equally in his image and yet different from each other, and this is not a fact to pretend blindness about but to honor and celebrate. The gospel does not make us colorblind. It frees us from being color *bound*. As such, ethnic justice, through the lens of the gospel, is about acknowledging the effects of the fall on racial distinctions (including the real existence and impacts of racism yesterday and today) and fully embracing the parity of all people bearing the *imago Dei*.

Christians may differ charitably on different means of achieving this parity, but we are not free to disregard the need for it altogether. Any kind of racial supremacy is basically heresy. And justice, according to the Scriptures, is essentially about bringing to bear God's righteousness. It is about applying the goodness of his holy law, which makes provisions both for suppressing wickedness and succoring the victims of it.

This is what is meant here by ethnic justice—the treating of all persons, including historically or contemporarily marginalized or underprivileged people groups, as equals as a reflection of the just God, who has made all persons equally in his image.

But what does this have to do with Galatians 2?

PETER'S SIN OF RACISM

This is how Paul recounts the problem:

> But when Cephas came to Antioch, I opposed him to his face, because he stood condemned. For before certain men came from James, he was eating with the Gentiles; but when they came he drew back and separated himself, fearing the circumcision party. And the rest of the Jews acted hypocritically along with him, so that even Barnabas was led astray by their hypocrisy. But when I saw that their conduct was not in step with the truth of the gospel, I said to Cephas before them all, "If you, though a Jew, live like a Gentile and not like a Jew, how can you force the Gentiles to live like Jews?" (Galatians 2:11–14)

To be clear, the immediate theological context is about food laws and circumcision. This is in large part Paul's thrust in the entire letter to the Galatian church, rebuking the Judaizer heresy and stumping for the soteriological foundation of *sola fide*. But there is an undeniable ethnic component to the matters of food laws and circumcision. It's not simply a theological debate. They cannot be separated from their contextual Jewishness, which means that associating these things with a superior righteousness is to associate Jewishness with a superior righteousness—and, consequently, non-Jewishness with an inferior one.

Paul brings up Peter's separating himself from gentiles (to play favorites) and forcing gentiles to follow Jewish customs (by implication) to rebuke Peter's circumstantial legalism, which is manifested in the sin of cultural partiality. In verse 15 he uses the phrases "Jews by birth" and "Gentile sinners" to bring up not just an apparent difference in theology but also an alleged difference in ethnicity/culture: "Jews are faithful. Gentiles are sinful." That's the assumed dynamic built on thousands of years of cultural and religious reinforcement that many Jewish believers subscribed to, which Paul confronts in verses 16–17 by saying that even Jews are not saved by their customs *but by their Christ*. It is faith that justifies, not religion. This makes Jew and gentile equal in both their sin and their Savior.

Paul makes this point perhaps more directly in Romans 9, where he distinguishes carefully between ethnic Israel and spiritual Israel, the children of physical descent and "the children of the promise" (v. 8). But ethnic parity is a serious component of both Christian mission in the days of the early church and apostolic teaching on unity in Christ. Jew-gentile unity is a tension point with all the weight of Isaiah's prophetic word on Israel's being a light to the nations (Isaiah 49:6) and all the eschatological vision of Revelation 5:9 at stake.

This is what makes Peter's favoritism so heinous. He isn't simply being snobby. He's engaging in ethnic discrimination. He is committing the sin of racism.

THE HISTORICAL RECORD

In our own tempestuous times, full of social justice warrior-ing and "wokeness," it has perhaps become fashionable to find racism where it does not exactly exist. The exegetical error of thrusting our own anxieties or suspicions back onto the text of Scripture is always a temptation for those seeking to wield some kind of authority in the heat of modern religious debates. But dismissing the impact of racism altogether is equally an error. And so we must see Peter's violation as one of ethnic favoritism, not merely falling into legalism.

Thomas Aquinas, for instance, repeatedly labels Peter's sin not as a reversion to trust in the dietary laws—in fact, he argues that Peter himself should know firsthand the theological error in that from his experience in Acts 10—but as a "separation from the Gentiles."[1] Likewise, in Martin Luther's classic commentary, he speaks of the complexity of Jew-gentile relations in their fullness. In relation to the confrontation recounted in Galatians 2, he writes, "It is evident that Paul is not speaking about ceremonies or the ceremonial law, as some people say, but about a far weightier matter—namely, the birth of the Jews."[2] He goes on to contrast Peter's aiding and abetting the belief that circumstantial trusting in Jewish heritage (and all that that entails) amounts to righteousness with actual faith in Christ.

In his volume on Galatians and Ephesians in the New Daily Study Bible, William Barclay depicts the ethnic tension as background for the passage this way:

---

1. Thomas Aquinas, *Commentary on Saint Paul's Epistle to the Galatians* (Albany, NY: Magi Books, 1966), 48–52.

2. Martin Luther, *Galatians* (Wheaton, IL: Crossway, 1998), 86.

The trouble was by no means at an end. Part of the life of the early Church was a common meal which they called the *Agape* or Love Feast. At this feast, the whole congregation came together to enjoy a common meal provided by pooling whatever resources they had. For many of the slaves, it must have been the only decent meal they had all week; and in a very special way, it marked the togetherness of the Christians.

That seems, on the face of it, a lovely thing. But we must remember the rigid exclusiveness of the more narrow-minded Jews who regarded their race as the chosen people in such a way as involved the rejection of all others. "The Lord is merciful and gracious" (Exodus 34:6; Psalm 2:5). "But he is only gracious to Israelites; other nations he will terrify." "The nations are as stubble or straw which shall be burned, or as chaff scattered to the wind." "If a man repents God accepts him, but that applies only to Israel and no other nation." "Love all but hate the heretics." This exclusiveness affected daily life. Strict Jews were forbidden even to do business with Gentiles; they must neither give hospitality to, nor accept hospitality from, Gentiles.[3]

More recently, New Testament scholar Tom Schreiner has remarked on the ethnic partiality evident in Peter's favoritism. For instance, in one of his important shorter critiques of the so-called New Perspective on Paul, he notes, "The new perspective has reminded us of a truth that could be easily forgotten. Jews and Gentiles are one in Christ. Ethnocentricism,

---

3. William Barclay, *The Letters to the Galatians and Ephesians* (Louisville: Westminster John Knox, 2002), 22–23.

racism, and exclusivism are contrary to the gospel."[4] This would be an odd thing for a stalwart of contemporary Reformed theology to say if Pauline justification had no entailments for ethnic pride or race.

It would be an error to see *justification proper*, whether articulated in Galatians or anywhere else in Scripture, as solely about ethnic inclusion, as some within the New Perspective appear to suggest. But you don't have to deny its racial implications to affirm the Protestant *sola* on which the church stands or falls. This is borne out further by Schreiner when he notes:

> The new perspective has actually, whether or not one agrees with its interpretation of works of law, reminded us of something very important here. The division between Jews and Gentiles, and the inclusion of the Gentiles was a very important theme for Paul. It is evident from reading Galatians, Romans, and Ephesians (which I take to be Pauline) that the inclusion of the Gentiles into the one people of God through Christ was a major issue for Paul.[5]

To be clear, Schreiner is not saying racial reconciliation is the prevailing theme of Paul or of Paul's concern in Galatians, only that we ought not deny the unity of Jews and gentiles as an implication of the gospel—a "major" one, in Schreiner's words.

Walter Hansen describes the ethnic context of Galatians 2 this way:

> It is important to note that Paul accuses Peter and the rest of the Jewish believers in Antioch of hypocrisy, not

---

4. Thomas R. Schreiner, "Another Look at the New Perspective," *The Southern Baptist Journal of Theology* 14.3 (2010): 16.

5. Schreiner, "Another Look," 6–7.

heresy: the rest of the Jews joined him in his hypocrisy (v. 13). Their action was inconsistent with their own
convictions about the truth of the gospel. They were
more influenced by their common racial identity as Jews
than by their new experience of unity in Christ with all
believers of every race.[6]

No, acknowledging the ethnic dimension to Peter's hypocrisy
in Galatians 2 is not a retrograde social gospel. It is in fact
the discounting of racial implications in the text that is the
modern innovation. The emphasis of ethnic discrimination
in Peter's sin has been noted further by scholars and preachers such as John Piper, Jarvis Williams, DeAron Washington,
Timothy Cho, and even John MacArthur, certainly no fan of
overemphasizing racism himself.[7] On the background of the
conflict in Galatians 2, MacArthur says: "So what you had was
the Jews holding to their own dietary laws and a kind of developing racism toward Gentiles. We saw the racism even in the
day of Jonah, where he didn't want to see Gentiles repent. Jews
resented, hated Gentiles; and they kept separate."[8] In his com-

---

6. G. Walter Hansen, *Galatians*, IVP New Testament Commentary (Downers Grove, IL: InterVarsity Press, 1994), 64.

7. John Piper, "Racial Diversity, Racial Harmony, and the Gospel Walk," sermon preached January 15, 2006, Desiring God, https://www.desiringgod.org/messages/racial-diversity-racial-harmony-and-the-gospel-walk; Jarvis J. Williams, "Racial Reconciliation, the Gospel, and the Church," *9Marks Journal* (Summer/Fall 2015), https://www.9marks.org/article/racial-reconciliation-the-gospel-and-the-church/; DeAron Washington, "What Racial Reconciliation Is Not: Racial Reconciliation Pt. 1," New Orleans Baptist Theological Seminary blog, February 6, 2017, https://www.nobts.edu/geauxtherefore/articles/2017/what-racial-reconciliation-is-not-racial-reconciliation-pt.-1.html; Timothy Cho, "Is Racism a Social Issue or a Gospel Issue?," Core Christianity, August 21, 2017, https://corechristianity.com/resource-library/articles/is-racism-a-social-issue-or-a-gospel-issue.

8. John MacArthur, "The Danger of Adding to the Gospel," sermon preached June 4, 2017, Grace to You, https://www.gty.org/library/sermons-library/48-9/the-danger-of-adding-to-the-gospel.

mentary, MacArthur suggests that Peter "still had remnants of prejudice against Gentiles."[9]

The sum of this evidence and more provides the exegetical case that what is informing Peter's hypocrisy is not merely a misunderstanding or category confusion about law and gospel. No, he is actually succumbing to the pressure of ethnic and cultural superiority. When this superiority is mixed into the church, the gospel is compromised. This is what Paul is concerned about. Thus the solution must be found in a right embracing of the good news.

THE SOLUTION IS THE GOSPEL (AND ALL OF ITS IMPLICATIONS)

Earlier in Galatians 2, Paul mentions how the apostles testing his ministry wanted to ensure his commitment to the poor. It may seem like an odd concern in what amounts to essentially a doctrinal examination. But the apostles, of course, were establishing what too many evangelicals today conveniently forget: that the gospel has implications for how we treat one another.

The ministry of Jesus Christ, which saves us, had a cultural and missiological context. The Scriptures that for thousands of years testified to him are a substantive foundation for understanding all of his works, both teaching and doing, in the four Gospels. And the extrapolation of his atoning work by the apostles in the rest of the New Testament represents an important "and then what?"—both for our thinking and our doing—which the Holy Spirit determined we should feed on as God's very words.

All of that is to say, Jesus did not come simply preaching the gospel as idea but the gospel as kingdom. One need only

---

9. John MacArthur, *Galatians* (Chicago: Moody, 1987), 50.

consider Paul's words in Romans 8 and 1 Corinthians 15 to see how expansive the finished work of Christ really is—just how much it is supposed to affect.

Thus, "just preach the gospel" is not an adequate solution to the problem of racism. While such a cry sounds gospel centered, it forgets that the real gospel has a multitude of implications that follow in the wake of belief.

What Paul says to Peter is basically this: "You are not in step with the truth of the gospel." The right walking was integral to the right affirmation. In other words, you can unsay with your actions what you say in your affirmations.

The gospel does not exist as an ideological abstraction. The gospel alone saves, yes. The gospel alone unites, yes. The gospel must be distinguished from its implications (lest we fall into the error of damnable legalism, which no doubt the social gospel is), but it should never be *divorced* from them. An implications-free gospel is merely a shibboleth, a theological golem built from the deadness of our self-comforting platitudes. The true gospel imputes to us the full righteousness of Christ and imparts to us the Spirit of obedience.

Let us return, then, to an earlier clarification: Galatians as a letter and *justification proper* are not about race. Paul's *ultimate* concern is the gospel: that no person is justified by anything—whether religion or race—except for faith alone in Christ alone. But there are very important implications for ethnic concerns in the Jew-gentile tension reflected in Galatians 2 and Paul's rebuke of Peter for exacerbating it. Paul is concerned that Peter know, that the Galatians know—and that *we* know—that ethnic justice, properly understood, is an entailment of the gospel.

If you want to see ethnic harmony in your church, pastor— if you want to see the unity *that can only be explained by the gospel*—you must fiercely proclaim justification by grace alone through faith alone in Christ alone, but you must also not be afraid to both call out ethnic disparities in the church when you see them and confront them with the better way of grace. The apostle Paul's recollection in Galatians 2 is our example and our mandate.

11 | Jamaal Williams

Reconciled under the Lordship of Christ

Ephesians 2:11–18

In 2015, an associate pastor of a majority-white congregation preached on Ephesians 2:11–18. While these verses were just the next ones in a sermon series on Ephesians, the pastor felt especially burdened about applying this text to his church because the community that the church was located in was low income and 55 percent African American. The pastor, along with the elders, thought that now was the time to challenge the church to take the next step in ethnic reconciliation by encouraging the congregation to pursue their neighbors in love.

When the pastor preached the sermon, the response was jarring. A few members walked out in the middle of it, others took to social media to complain, and some confronted him afterward. The pastor described it as spiritual warfare. He said that, more than any other sermon that he had preached before, he could feel the heaviness of each word.

A year after that sermon was preached, this church called me to be the lead pastor and the first African American on staff in its sixteen-year history.[1] Since the Ephesians 2 sermon

---

1. To learn more about this sermon and my experience with coming to Sojourn Church Midtown, listen to "Where the Gospel Meets Racial Reconciliation,"

and the hiring of an African American lead pastor, Sojourn Church Midtown has grown significantly in diversity. Where the church had only one minority on staff in its history, it currently has eight nonwhite employees. These employees include Asian, Latino, Haitian, and African American brothers and sisters. While the church has a long way to go, the culture has shifted. It has become more integrated and is becoming accessible for people of all ethnicities and cultures.

In this chapter, I provide an aerial view of how to preach and apply Ephesians 2:11–18 along with practical wisdom to consider when preaching it. The audience I have in mind is the pastor whose congregation is at the beginning of its journey regarding preaching on ethnic reconciliation. Moreover, this chapter is tailored to address the divide between the black church and the white church in America since it is one of the, if not the, most profound ethnic divides in America. Also, I address this divide because of the significant ethnic turmoil that erupted in the aftermath of the killing of George Floyd in May 2020. For more information about this ethnic divide and the American church's complicity and role in it, read *Divided by Faith* by Michael O. Emerson and Christian Smith, and *Doctrine and Race* by Mary Beth Swetnam Mathews.[2]

INTERPRETING THE PASSAGE

In Ephesians, Paul addresses "faithful saints" who live in the major metropolitan area of Ephesus (1:1).[3] Throughout his letter, he is addressing both Jewish and gentile Christians,

---

Love Thy Neighborhood, January 17, 2017, https://lovethyneighborhood.org/episode-1-racial-reconciliation.

2. Michael O. Emerson and Christian Smith, *Divided by Faith: Evangelical Religion and the Problem of Race in America* (Oxford: Oxford University Press, 2000); Mary Beth Swetnam Mathews, *Doctrine and Race: African American Evangelicals and Fundamentalism between the Wars* (Tuscaloosa: University of Alabama Press, 2018).

3. Bible quotations in this chapter are from the Christian Standard Bible.

though it appears that the majority are gentile. A strong theme of the book of Ephesians is that Christ is reconciling all creation under his lordship and saving both Jew and gentile by grace through faith (Ephesians 2–4). As a result, we can live together in unity as Christ's church.

THROUGH CHRIST, GENTILE CHRISTIANS HAVE BEEN "BROUGHT NEAR"

After richly encouraging both Jewish and gentile Christians by pointing them to their adoption in Christ, in 2:11–14 Paul builds up gentile Christians. He does this by reminding them that they have equal standing in the body of Christ to their Jewish brothers and sisters.

In the entire book of Ephesians, Paul takes on the tone of a father lavishing encouragement on a younger child who feels like he doesn't have a place in the family because of the success of an older sibling. It's as if the father is saying, "You have the same place in our family; everyone is equally valued; we are one." In chapter 1, Paul reminds Jewish and gentile Christians of how they have been blessed with every spiritual blessing in heaven and chosen before the foundation of the world (1:3–4). In 2:1–10, Paul reminds both Jewish and gentile Christians that they were dead in their trespasses and sins and that God made them alive in Christ Jesus by grace through faith. Both groups are equally God's workmanship (2:10). For first-century gentile Christians, to be assured that they were adopted into the family of God before the foundation of the world, just as Jewish Christians were, would have been no small thing.

In 2:11–14, Paul fleshes out for the gentiles why grace is so amazing by reminding them how alienated they were before they accepted Christ. They were:

- called "the uncircumcised" (circumcision was a sign of having a covenantal relationship with Israel's God),

- "excluded from the citizenship of Israel," and

- "foreigners to the covenants of promise."

As a result of these truths, Gentiles were "without hope and without God in the world" (2:12).

However, in Ephesians 2:13 we are interrupted with a "but": "But now in Christ Jesus, you who were far away have been brought near by the blood of Christ." The simplicity and beauty of the phrase "you who were far away [gentiles] have been brought near by the blood of Christ" reminds me of the power and simplicity of the old African American hymn written by Evelyn Simpson, "I Know It Was the Blood." The opening stanza and refrain say:

> I know it was the blood,
> I know it was the blood,
> I know it was the blood for me.
> One day when I was lost
> he died upon the cross.
> I know it was the blood for me.

It is through the blood of Jesus that gentiles have been brought near. They have not been brought near through circumcision, covenants, or any other Jewish practices—as beautiful as they were! Paul shows that it is only through Christ's blood that both Jews and gentiles become found and adopted into the family of God.

THROUGH THE CROSS OF
CHRIST, THE WALL OF HOSTILITY
HAS BEEN TORN DOWN

The key to racial reconciliation and multiethnic ministry has been handed to the church through the nail-pierced palms of Christ. In Ephesians 2:14–15, Paul makes this point clear by emphasizing that peace comes through the cross of Christ.

It's common knowledge that in the Jerusalem temple there was a literal barrier that stopped gentiles from entering the inner courts where Israel worshiped. However, while Paul's words may have reminded Jewish Christians of this reality, most gentile Christians may not have identified quickly with such a reference. More than likely, when Paul references the dividing wall of hostility, he is referring to the law (v. 15). Frank Thielman writes:

> The focus of 2:11–22 is the social alienation between Israel and the Gentiles and Christ's role in solving this problem through his death, which set aside the Mosaic law, with its tendency to divide Jews from Gentiles. Although the death of Christ also overcomes the hostility between God and humanity, this element of the passage serves the passage's more prominent theme of the peace that now exists between Jews and Gentiles. By overcoming the hostility between God and all human beings, Christ's death breaks down the wall of hostility between Jews and Gentiles.[4]

Christ brought peace by creating one new man from the two, Paul writes. Jesus put to death the hostility between Jews and gentiles, by submitting himself to death on the cross. The Holy Spirit uses this good news of peace to empower us to pursue

---

4. Frank Thielman, *Ephesians*, Baker Exegetical Commentary on the New Testament (Grand Rapids: Baker Academic, 2010), 148.

peace with each other (vv. 16–18). When gentile Christians and Jewish Christians believe and live out of this truth, they no longer live like foreigners and strangers but grow as one household and temple with their Jewish brothers and sisters.

Ever since the fall, we see division among people. This division can be seen in Adam and Eve hiding their bodies in shame and in Cain murdering his brother for giving an acceptable sacrifice (see Genesis 3–4). Life in the first Adam allows differences to divide, but life in the second Adam sees differences as an opportunity to unify and create something beautiful for the glory of God. Through the gospel, the church can have peace because she worships the Prince of Peace. Jesus has torn down the dividing wall of hostility by allowing his flesh to be torn into pieces. The cross of Christ shapes the way we see ethnic reconciliation and enables us to walk in unity.

APPLYING THE PASSAGE

I've preached and taught Ephesians 2:11–18 many times. A few times, I've preached this sermon in mostly white contexts. Once, I later learned that not only was I the first African American to teach at a particular white church, but also the first African American to preach in the history of any church in that community. Each time I have preached this sermon, the body of Christ has been edified, but some people were also offended. You must consider the cost.

As you apply a sermon on this passage, I encourage you regardless of the context to help the congregation see that Paul was encouraging the gentile Christians by reminding them of their place in the body of Christ. There is not a one-to-one correlation between Jew-gentile hostility and black/white hostility, so any parallels between the two situations should be made with nuance. One parallel is that, because of the history of racism and injustice toward blacks in this country, black Christians, like gentile Christians, must be encouraged and valued within the church in America. Black Christians need this encouragement and valuing precisely because their experience with white Christians has often been paternalistic in nature.

When I apply Ephesians 2, I encourage white brothers and sisters toward a posture of humility and action (remember that my intended audience for this chapter is the pastor whose congregation is at the beginning of its journey toward reconciliation, specifically with the white-black divide). There are many possible applications of Ephesians 2, but they fall into two main categories. The first is a call to be broken and the second a call to be bold.

Here are a few suggested ways to call your hearers to be broken:

- Lament the sufferings of African Americans in our nation's history. The year 2019 marked the four hundredth year of African slaves in America. The majority of our experience in America has been under unjust laws (the institution of slavery, Jim Crow, both de facto and de jure housing laws, etc.). And, while the African American community has communal sins and vices, like every community, this should not stop you from weeping with us as we weep because of historical injustices.

- Point out that, as a result of laws and widespread practices such as redlining, unfair housing practices, privatized prisons, the GI Bill and its implementation, and unjust law practices, the African American community has been crippled socially and economically.

- Say that, on top of this, the American church has been complicit in the ethnic divide along the way. The church has ignored abolitionists and pastors from the very beginning who warned America of the atrocities and sinfulness of slavery.

- Repent of personal prejudices and racism.

- Weep because of apathy and a turning of the eye away from justice.

Once you have called your hearers to be broken, you should also call them to be bold. Here are a few suggested ways to do that:

- Be clear that confronting racism addresses a stronghold, and they will inevitably face backlash.

- Point out that boldness includes confronting prejudices, personal preferences, and sinful attitudes toward African Americans in particular, and any disunity among people in general. You can use illustrations here from your own life if you have confronted family members or others making racist comments.

- Encourage members to look for opportunities to serve the poor, fatherless, marginalized, and oppressed by using their power and privilege to affect others (Psalm 82:12–12; James 1:27).

- Provide examples from our nation's history that may be new to your hearers. Normally in my sermon on Ephesians 2:11–18, I bring up African American

Christian history that most whites haven't heard in order to show how slanted most Americans' understanding of history is. I introduce names such as George Lisle, Absalom Jones, Richard Allen, and Lott Carey. Perhaps here you can recommend a biography of an African American Christian that you've read and learned from. Also, you can challenge your congregants to start reading authors of different ethnicities.

CONCLUSION

Finally, remember that sermons are just one part of an overall ministry strategy of reconciliation. Shepherd your people and give them a healthy vision of what reconciliation could look like—which may require you to reach out to an African American pastor to ask for advice and research best practices. This could also mean that, after seeking the Lord in prayer and in community, you should also speak up when the African American community is preyed on in matters related to justice.

Be intentional to step out of your comfort zone to befriend minorities, submit to African American leadership, and learn from African American preachers. Intentionally use your knowledge and position to empower African Americans who are marginalized. And always remember that you are a sign and not a solution, and that you are running a marathon and not a sprint.

Preaching this text will mean that you have not only to exegete the text, but your audience and, more importantly, your own heart. This risk of preaching the word poignantly is great, but the reward of obeying Jesus and pushing against the stronghold of racism in our country is greater.

The Chosen People and Racial Reconciliation

1 Peter 2:9

I was nineteen years old when I filled my first ministry role in a local church. Looking back, I was much too young—not just in years but also in the faith. Still, because the Lord used high school students to bring me to himself, I wanted to work with that age group. So, during my freshman year at the University of Florida, I served as the youth and music director of a rural church outside Gainesville. One Sunday, I invited a friend to play the piano and sing during our morning service. At the end of the service, the pastor pulled me aside, put his arms around me, and said, "Juan, I appreciate what you're trying to do, but please don't do it again." The problem? She was black. It never entered my mind that inviting her would be an issue.

During my senior year at Florida, I served in a similar role at another rural church. To encourage our families, I published a monthly newsletter. One afternoon, the mother of a teenage student complained about that month's newsletter. In it, I had painted an African American celebrity in a positive light. She warned that if I continued doing that, young people would grow tolerant of "mixed-race" relationships. When I reminded her that I, a Puerto Rican, had married an Anglo American, she told me I was "white" because there are only three races.

After graduating from university, my wife and I, with one child in tow, moved to Georgia so I could serve as a student minister at a church. Through the generous donation of a member, we installed outdoor basketball hoops to reach local youth. As it began to attract more people, a prominent deacon who was also a friend took me aside and asked, "What will you do if they want to come to church?" I was confused. "Isn't that the whole point?" The deacon was afraid that if the young African American males began attending the predominantly Anglo church, the black kids and the white kids would become romantically involved.

It is a grievous indictment against the church that the very people called to display to an unbelieving world God's reconciling work on the cross of Christ (Ephesians 3:10) instead display the same ethnic divisions as the rest of fallen humanity. Thankfully, not every church is characterized by such blatant discrimination, but one prejudiced church is one too many. How did we arrive at this point? For generations, Americans have been discipled in a vision of racial discrimination. That's not to say that all white people are racists. That's a lazy argument. Still, it is naive to ignore how a simple review of American history reveals a failure to address the issue of race-based discrimination: slavery was accepted during the revolutionary period; the issue of slavery was avoided in the constitutional convention; the Civil War changed no one's mind; Reconstruction changed no one's hearts; Jim Crow laws legalized discrimination; and civil rights were granted reluctantly to blacks. To this day, racial division exists in our culture and in too many of our churches.

The solution for the racial divide is the same as the problem—discipleship. We overcome wrong, distorted, sinful visions of the church by replacing them with a right, clear, biblical vision. This is what it means to renew your mind—to replace old, sinful ways of thinking with new, gospel ways of thinking (Ephesians 4:20–24). While all Scripture serves as a source for the renewal of the mind, allow me to offer a picture of the church from 1 Peter 2:9. I pray that this vision of the people of God will help us renew our thinking about who we are in Christ—a people chosen out of the world to display the kingdom of God on the earth and call all peoples everywhere to repent of their sins and bow down to our King.

WE ARE A CHOSEN RACE

Race-based discrimination begins with the lie that one race is superior to another or to all others. The Bible, on the other hand, clarifies that there is only one race, the human race, and that all human beings are equal as God's image (Genesis 1:26–28).[1] Additionally, after the fall, we are equally guilty before a holy God (Romans 5:12–21). The gospel reminds us, though, that God is at work, in Christ, to gather a people for himself out of all the ethnicities of the world. We are a *chosen* race—"elect exiles of the Dispersion" (1 Peter 1:1), chosen "according to the foreknowledge of God" (1:2). In the Bible, foreknowledge is not simple knowledge before the fact; it is intimate knowledge before time (1:20; see Ephesians 1:4). The basis of our election, then, is not according to any intrinsic worth or merit. It is solely grounded in God's free choice to express his covenant love to a particular people. On what basis, then, may we think

---

1. For more on Genesis 1:27 and the image of God, see Matthew D. Kim's chapter in this book.

of ourselves as better than others based on our ethnicity, culture, or even social standing? We can't. At least, not on biblical grounds. We are God's people chosen out of all the peoples of the world for his own possession. To what end?

Well, as a chosen *race*, we are a new humanity. Out of the old, sinful humanity, God is creating a new one, chosen to "proclaim the excellencies of him who called you out of darkness into his marvelous light" (1 Peter 2:9). That phrase is a direct reference to Isaiah 43:20–21, and Peter applies it to the church. Isaiah 43 recounts God's promise to redeem exiled Israel through a second exodus that will be far greater than the first (Isaiah 43:18–19). To be sure, the initial reference to "my chosen people" in Isaiah 43 is to Israel, Abraham's biological offspring. The Greek translation of Isaiah 43:20 in the Septuagint bears this out, translating the Hebrew as "my chosen race" (*genos*). But the New Testament reveals that Jesus is the answer to Israel's exile (Matthew 1:1–17). Jesus is God, the incarnate Son, who began the new exodus (Matthew 2:15), passing through the waters of the Jordan River (Matthew 3:13–17) and retracing Israel's wilderness wandering (Matthew 4:1–2). Unlike Israel, though, Jesus kept the covenant (Matthew 4:3–11). As the new and better Moses, he gave the new law (Matthew 5–7). And as the promised King from David's line, he re-formed the people of God on the foundation of the twelve apostles (Matthew 10:1–42; 16:13–20; 19:27–28; Revelation 21:14). Having ratified the new covenant with his blood as the faithful priest (Matthew 26:26–29; 1 Peter 1:2), Jesus is now gathering a people to God from every tribe and language and nation—the people whom the Father has chosen. This is the new humanity. This is the church. This is us.

While Israel was a chosen race in a genealogical sense, the church, composed of both Jews and gentiles, is a new race, chosen by God out of the world to become the people of God through faith (obedience to Jesus Christ—1 Peter 1:2). As a new race, we can no longer separate ourselves according to ethnicity or affinity, for we are one in Christ (Galatians 3:27–29). As a new humanity, our primary identity is not our ethnicity (Jew/gentile) or gender (male/female) or age (young/old) or status (rich/poor); our primary identity is in Christ. It's not that our ethnicity or gender are eradicated when we come to faith in Christ—I am and always will be a Puerto Rican male, but I am a new creation in Christ. But, because of the human need for acceptance and belonging, we are tempted to identify primarily along ethnic, cultural, generational, gender, even socioeconomic lines. And, because of sin, pride, hatred, and partiality drive us further apart. The church, though, is a countercultural community, a new race composed of a diversity of peoples who have been united by a Jewish King. In this new humanity, our love for one another proves we belong to Christ (John 13:34–35); our unity proves that the Father sent the Son (John 17:21); and our life together proves that our God is wise (Ephesians 3:10). But, if we do not love our brothers and sisters in Christ, *all* of them, we prove that we don't know God (1 John 4:8).

Though there are countless ways we might display God's wisdom and glory as a chosen race, at the very least, our churches should reflect the diversity of the communities in which we live. That means that as the neighborhoods around our churches change, so should the makeup of our membership. What does it say of us when we seek the reconciliation of the races but, instead of welcoming Christians of differing ethnicities into our churches, we plant an ethnic church for those who are different than we are or simply relocate our congregation to a more comfortable environment? God is greatly magnified as wise when a local church reflects the diversity of peoples in its locale and when they live together as sons and daughters of the Father. Admittedly, there may not be much ethnic diversity in the neighborhood where your church is located, but there are other kinds of diversity: socio-economic, gender, generational. So, as we plan our Sunday services, we should be asking, Is there anything we do when we gather that unnecessarily excludes Christians who are different than we are? Imagine the powerful picture we provide to the world and heaven and hell when male and female, rich and poor, black and white, Asian and Hispanic, educated and uneducated, CEO and custodian all come to the Lord's Table as one. Let the world celebrate diversity; we will celebrate *unified* diversity. And we do this not just for our sake, but for the sake of the world.

WE ARE A ROYAL PRIESTHOOD

Because we are united with Christ, we are *royal* sons and daughters who share in God's *rule* (Revelation 1:5–6; 2:26–27; 3:21; 20:4). Until Christ's kingdom is fully revealed in the consummation, we are God's royal representatives, displaying his rule over the earth. Since we have royal status, it should not matter what this world says of us. It should not matter what rights or privileges they take away from us. We are royalty, and no one or nothing can strip us of our identity in Christ! Why, then, would we discriminate against one another? Why would we think of ourselves as better (or less) than someone else?

But we're not just royal; we're also priestly. Priests have special access to God. Under the old covenant, only the priests were permitted to serve in God's presence in the temple. But now a new temple has been erected. We are the living stones of this new temple, being constructed on the foundation of Christ (1 Peter 2:4–8). And as God promised to reside in the old temple, he also dwells in the new temple by his Spirit. As those indwelt by the Spirit of God, we have special access to the presence of God. *All* of us. How, then, could we exclude from our gatherings those whom the Father welcomes? My sister in Christ, whom I invited to sing in the congregation, was a fellow priest, called to offer spiritual sacrifices of praise (1 Peter 2:5; Hebrews 13:15). She is welcome in God's presence. She should have been welcomed in ours as well.

But we do not enjoy God's presence for our own sake; we serve in God's presence for the sake of the world. That is, as priests, we also have a mediatorial role. To be sure, "there is only one mediator between God and men, the man Christ Jesus" (1 Timothy 2:5). But, as priests in Christ, one of the primary ways we represent God to the world is by proclaiming his lordship over all things and calling all peoples everywhere to bow the knee to King Jesus and worship him. So, even our evangelism must be multiethnic and multicultural because the people God is gathering are from every tribe and nation and language. Not only must we welcome all peoples into our churches, then, but we must also pursue all peoples with the gospel. My deacon friend was concerned about an African American young man catching his daughter's eye. His greater concern should have been to fulfill his role as a priest, proclaiming the gospel of the King so that those young men playing basketball might have had an opportunity to embrace Christ and become his followers. And the best thing that could have happened to his daughter in the realm of dating was to meet a young Christian man who would marry her and love her as Christ loves the church—regardless of his skin color.

WE ARE A HOLY NATION

God chose us out of this world, made us a new race, and gave us royal status. Consequently, we are distinct from the world. As God chose Israel and made them distinct from the surrounding nations in their worship, their government, their sexual ethic, and even their diet and clothing, we are also a new humanity chosen from the world to be distinct from the world.

However, unlike Israel, a nation established in a central geographical location, the church is a nation established on "Mount Zion ... the heavenly Jerusalem" (Hebrews 12:22) and manifested throughout the world in local assemblies. Our citizenship is in heaven, but, as a royal priesthood and holy nation, we represent God's kingdom on earth as his ambassadors. That means that as unbelievers in our communities look at the church, they should be witnessing God's people, chosen out of all the peoples of the world, living together as brothers and sisters in Christ. They should witness the love of God expressed in our care for one another. They should witness the justice of the kingdom expressed in our midst. For we are sojourners in this world, representing King Jesus—showing the world what it is like to live under his just rule and gracious blessing, so that the world "may see your good deeds and glorify God on the day of visitation" (1 Peter 2:12). The world's calls for racial reconciliation should not be an indictment against the church. Instead, when unbelievers call for reconciliation, they should look at us and see love, not hate; unity, not division; reconciliation, not discrimination.

CONCLUSION

As a royal priesthood and holy nation, chosen out of the world to be a new humanity, we show the world who our God is, what he is like, and what it is like to live under his rule and blessing. We are to be a holy people mediating God's gifts to the world. And we are to call all peoples everywhere to turn away from their sin, including hatred, discrimination, and division, and bow down to King Jesus in faith. A day is coming when every knee will bow and every tongue will confess that Jesus Christ is Lord. Until that day, we are God's people chosen out of the world to represent him on this earth and to deliver his message to the world.

Racial Reconciliation and the Victory of Christ

Revelation 5:9–10

The book of Revelation is a strange book, full of stark and startling images. It is written in a genre called apocalyptic, which emerged in the midst of trouble and persecution, and which tries to point us beyond present circumstances to hope in God's victory over evil. Contrary to popular usage, the word "apocalypse" does not refer to the end of the world per se, but to an unveiling or disclosure of things that are otherwise hidden. This disclosure comes from God, usually through angelic intermediaries, to a human figure who is then responsible to communicate the vision more widely.[1] Christians past and present have differing preconceptions of what the book of Revelation is and what it means. For many, the book encourages speculation about the end times. In my judgment, a more edifying approach for preachers is to discourage such speculation and to instead emphasize the book's call to faithfulness, its assurance of hope, and its invitation to worship God in Christ.

---

1. See Bart D. Erhman, *A Brief Introduction to the New Testament* (New York: Oxford University Press, 2017), 341–44 for a description of apocalyptic literature, both in the Bible and outside it.

This approach to the book of Revelation—call it exhortative instead of speculative—is a much more fruitful one for preachers, particularly when considering issues of racial reconciliation. Too many approaches to Revelation emphasize future fulfillment while downplaying the text's call to faithfulness *now*. Given the renewed urgency for racial reconciliation—as evidenced by protests against police violence against African Americans or ongoing calls for Indigenous self-determination, to cite but two examples—there is a need for preachers to boldly speak God's word to contemporary concerns in distinctly Christian terms. After all, the answer to any issue the church faces, whether on race or anything else, is Jesus Christ, true God and true man. Christian preaching must remain resolutely Christological, lest the church lose its scriptural bearings and float aimlessly on the seas of cultural change. In what follows I will take up Revelation 5:9–10 and, through exegesis and contemporary application, suggest some ways the text can bring the light of the gospel to bear on issues of racial justice and reconciliation.

A word of warning up front: As preachers, we must tread carefully with the book of Revelation, especially if we're dealing with conflict and division, racial or otherwise. Since the book depicts a stark dualism of good versus evil, we have to be careful we don't use it simply to reinforce our own biases such that we are the "good guys" and others we disapprove of are the "bad guys." This has the potential to inflame conflicts of various kinds and indeed has done so throughout history.[2] That said, if

---

2. Even if it is a little hyperbolic, Elaine Pagels has a valid point: "Ever since, Christians have adapted [John's] visions to changing times, reading their own social, political, and religious conflict into the cosmic war he so powerfully evokes. Perhaps most startling is how Constantine invoked John's vision of Christ's victory over Rome to endorse his own imperial rule. More than a thousand years later, Lutherans published Lucas Cranach's pictures of the pope as the whore of Babylon in one of the first Lutheran Bibles, while an early Catholic biographer retaliated by depicting Luther,

we keep the vision of Christ from Revelation 5 at the forefront, we are more likely to remain centered on the gospel.

THE HYMN OF ALL CREATION

In the fourth and fifth chapters of the book of Revelation we are drawn, along with John, into heaven. John, in a vision, stands before an open door, and the voice of Jesus invites him to step through and experience heavenly realities that are beyond human imagining (4:1). These two chapters are the center of the book. Everything moves toward them and flows from them.

Upon entering the open door, John finds himself in God's throne room. The scene is full of rich biblical imagery and symbolism: precious stones, a rainbow, thunder and lightning, torches, the number seven, the number twelve, living creatures with many eyes and wings who sing praise to the holy God. All of these are figures directing us back to Sinai, to the temple, to visions of the prophets Isaiah and Ezekiel. These rich biblical images coalesce in the revelation of Jesus Christ, who is both "Lion of Judah" (5:5) and slaughtered Lamb (5:6). Again, more figures here: we are reminded of Davidic kingship, founded on God's covenant (2 Samuel 7) and established and upheld "with justice and with righteousness" (Isaiah 9:7) by God's Messiah.[3] We are also reminded of the Passover (Exodus 12), which is brought to completion because "our paschal lamb, Christ, has been sacrificed" (1 Corinthians 5:7). What keeps these biblical

on the frontispiece, as the seven-headed beast. During the catastrophic times of the American Civil War, Confederate loyalists portrayed Lincoln being strangled by the great dragon that is the Union, while those on the Union side took as their war anthem 'Battle Hymn of the Republic,' which weaves Jeremiah's and John's prophecies into that war, now seen as the Great Tribulation that precedes God's final judgment." Elaine Pagels, *Revelations: Visions, Prophecy and Politics in the Book of Revelation* (New York: Viking, 2012), 173–74.

3. Scripture quotations in this chapter are from the New Revised Standard Version.

threads from turning into a tangle is the way God's justice and sacrificial mercy are embodied in Jesus Christ. It takes homiletical skill to communicate the force of this imagery without getting bogged down in tedious explanatory details. The power of this scene lies in the way the imagery, taken together, expresses the juxtaposition between God's glorious presence and Christ's sacrificial death. That juxtaposition takes us to the heart of the gospel, because it reveals the identity of our Lord, both victor and victim, sacrifice and priest, king and slave. Is it any surprise, then, that only Jesus Christ is "worthy to take the scroll and to open its seals" (Revelation 5:9)? This is the meaning of the world, of history, of Scripture: that Christ has fulfilled all the purposes of God, has given up his life for the world's salvation, and has established God's rule "on earth as it is in heaven" (Matthew 6:10).

And now, our text: Revelation 5:9–10 is a hymn sung by the four living creatures and the twenty-four elders. The living creatures each have a different face—lion, ox, human, eagle—which have variously been understood to refer to different aspects of the created order, to the four evangelists who authored the Gospels, or to the kingly, priestly, incarnational, and pneumatic work of Jesus Christ.[4] The twenty-four elders represent the unity

---

4. These options can be seen in the quotations from church fathers in W. C. Weinrich, ed., *Revelation*, Ancient Christian Commentary on Scripture (Downers Grove, IL: InterVarsity Press, 2005), 62–66. Admittedly, this typological or "figural" way of reading the Bible is unfamiliar for many modern Christians. However, it was common in previous eras, and there is a contemporary movement that broadly goes under the umbrella of "theological interpretation of Scripture" that seeks to revive it. This is, in part, a reaction to the way historical-critical methods of reading the Bible have dominated in recent centuries, but it is primarily driven by theological considerations rather than methodological ones. In my judgment this is a welcome development for preachers, because it conceives of Scripture as a rich and dynamic web of interconnected things, produced and taken up by God in his creative work of revealing, concealing, making, and unmaking—ever new and always surprising. For further reading, see Ephraim Radner, *Time and the World: The Figural Reading of the Christian Scriptures* (Grand Rapids: Eerdmans, 2016); Christopher R. Seitz, *Figured Out: Typology and Providence in Christian Scripture* (Louisville: Westminster John

of the Old and New Testaments, along with the twelve tribes of Israel, embodying the patriarchs and the law and the prophets, and the twelve apostles, embodying the church of Jesus Christ.[5] Taken together, Christ is being praised by all creation, by all the saints throughout time, and by all the words of holy Scripture. Again, don't bury your listeners under an avalanche of imagery here. Use it to point to Christ and let your listeners make the connections.

The primary focus of the hymn is what Jesus Christ has accomplished for us by his death. He has "ransomed for God saints from every tribe and language and people and nation" (5:9). This is a fulfillment of God's covenantal promise to Abraham that "in you all the families of the earth shall be blessed" (Genesis 12:3). It is also a fulfillment of the exodus, in which God ransoms the Israelites from slavery by the blood of the lamb (Genesis 12:1–13; 1 Peter 1:18–20). The costly sacrifice of the Lamb of God has not only freed us from slavery to sin and death, but has also drawn the various peoples of the earth together and bound them in his justice and love. This is a miraculous achievement, something only God can accomplish. Utopian projects, from Babel to Marx, have tried to unite the peoples of the world on purely human terms but have always failed.

CALLED TO MAKE
THE VICTORY VISIBLE

Despite the force of John's vision, we must admit that the work of Christian unity is far from finished and is often scandalously deficient. Much of the time we don't look like people who have

---

Knox, 2001). For an excellent treatment of figural reading as it pertains to preaching, see Annette Brownlee, *Preaching Jesus Christ Today: Six Questions for Moving from Scripture to Sermon* (Grand Rapids: Baker Academic), 2018.

    5. See Weinrich, *Revelation*, 60–61.

been ransomed and bound together in Christian love. The church has too often contributed to human division and disintegration, often in horrific ways (there is no need to rehearse the many examples here). As preachers, we must face these realities honestly. Triumphalism in the pulpit helps no one. After all, the book of Revelation, like so much of Scripture, upholds the victory of Christ while plainly acknowledging conflict, persecution, temptation, and trouble. Even the most faithful members of our congregations come with anxieties and sins and strained relationships. The gospel speaks to all of that, so we should not avoid difficult topics in the pulpit, particularly when these topics are important personally and culturally.

So how can we address issues of race from this passage? We use the term "race" as a modern synonym for older categorizations such as "tribe and language and people and nation." To speak of race is to speak of *difference*, of the various characteristics that differentiate one human being from another. To describe a person as "black" or "Indigenous" is to say that this person embodies certain distinctives that mark them off from other human beings who don't embody those same distinctives. From a Christian perspective, these distinctives are not deficiencies but evidence of God's will to show forth his truth, goodness, and beauty in the things he has made. Multiethnic, multicultural, and multilingual churches are visible signs of God's creativity and sacrificial love. In other words, for Christians racial differences ought to be celebrated rather than treated as a problem. Christian unity does not erase or downplay differences, but instead binds us together in the love of Christ. Why else would Revelation 5:9–10 make a point of describing racially and culturally diverse Christians worshiping *together*?

Nevertheless, racism, which is injustice arising from racial discrimination, remains a real and pervasive reality in our world, in both explicit and implicit ways. Western culture has tended to increasingly highlight implicit racial discrimination as an ongoing problem, such as the way one's racial identity denotes certain "privileges" that are often unseen or unacknowledged. These issues are complex, far too complex to explore in any depth here, but suffice it to say that racism—that is, willful hatred and discrimination toward people who are "different"—is a betrayal of Christ and a rejection of the gospel. Racial reconciliation is not a marginal element of our faith. It is our destiny as people joined to Christ and in Christ. Preachers would do well to point that out, often and clearly.

These are matters the church must continue to attend to, but on its own terms and within its own biblical worldview rather than following the confused and confusing judgments of the culture. Preachers must be careful here, as the desire to appear relevant or "woke" can lead us to simply parrot the ideas of the cultural elite as expressed in mass media. The Christian contribution to these issues can never be a mere replica of secular priorities, because Christ's call to repentance and life in the Spirit is more demanding than any of that. Simply put, Christ calls us to take up our cross, to love our neighbor as ourselves, and to strive for spiritual perfection (not the kind of thing you hear from National Public Radio!).

This text, then, opens up a paradox for us, which is the objective victory of Christ over the powers of darkness and division, and the ongoing call for us to make that victory visible in our lives and in our communities. We don't add to Christ's victory, but we do have a role in making it evident to others. This goes to the purpose of redemption—not as an end in itself, but as the beginning of a process of growing into Christlikeness. When God rescued Israel from Egypt, he didn't just send them on their way, free from slavery and now able to do as they please. No, *he made something of them.* Just so, Christ has made something of us. He has made us "a kingdom and priests serving our God" (Revelation 5:10). Racial reconciliation in the church—that is, diverse people bound together in Christian love—is a visible manifestation of Christ's victory over everything that opposes God. Preachers have a responsibility here to help move these concerns to the center of Christian thinking and acting, and preaching on them from Scripture can help to do that. Western forms of Christianity, particularly free-church traditions, often downplay ecclesiology, so this can be part of a broader homiletical strategy to help Christians see themselves as part of the body of Christ rather than simply as an individual person in relationship to Christ.

CONCLUSION

I began by suggesting we preach Revelation in an exhortative way rather than a speculative way. Speculation on eschatological fulfillment can entirely direct our attention away from the present world and its troubles, which is not the point of this book. Yes, our only hope lies beyond our world, in Christ's ultimate victory, but to confess that does not require us to turn a blind eye to present troubles. Rather, it helps us reframe present troubles so that whatever difficulties we face are all seen as temporal, in contrast to the eternal reality of Christ's kingdom.

That said, many in our congregations will have strong opinions on Revelation. Some may not welcome an approach that downplays eschatological speculation. Skilled preachers know their own context and will decide how best to teach this in a way that will not alienate or shut down our listeners, but invite them to see the text in a new way. We should not be rigid about this; after all, future fulfillment—especially Christ's second coming—is central to Christian hope. What we want to avoid is any approach that denies or obscures present struggles as a way of avoiding uncomfortable realities.

The image of "saints from every tribe and language and people and nation" gathered together is a powerful one. How we preach on this depends on our context. Preachers in multi-ethnic congregations can positively highlight and celebrate the way their people are already on the right track, and encourage them to continue modeling the reconciliation that the gospel both demands and looks forward to eschatologically. Preachers in less diverse contexts can perhaps challenge and remind their congregations that Christ's body is a very diverse reality and that this is God's intention. One way to do this is to tell congregants about the growth of the church in the Global South in the twentieth century, which may be a surprise to some of our people.[6]

Preachers in contexts where racial tension and conflict is present have a difficult job. Knowing something of the history of these tensions and conflicts is important. Not all racial tension is driven by explicit racism. In some places, socioeconomic factors drive suspicion and hostility. Other places have histories of cultural dislocation, perhaps arising from colonialism, and this has led to resentment and distrust. In contexts that are multicultural and multilingual, there may be lingering unease about "the other," whereby people don't know how to relate to one another and feel the chasm between them is too vast to bridge. Again, the cause of division is key here, and preachers need to know their people. We help no one if we clumsily or pedantically venture into relational dynamics that we barely understand. Get to know people, hear their stories, learn the history. Often what is unsaid is most important.

---

6. A good book on this topic is Philip Jenkins, *The Next Christendom: The Coming of Global Christianity* (Oxford: Oxford University Press, 2011).

That said, if explicit racism is present in the congregation, then some kind of prophetic witness is likely needed. This takes great courage and wisdom. It takes courage to say difficult things from the pulpit, and it takes wisdom to say it at the right time and in the right way. What is most necessary here is that opposition to racism is spoken in the context of the gospel. In other words, racism is insidious because it undermines the work of Christ and obscures our vision of him. Racism is sin, but it is not an unforgivable sin. The remedy, then, is repentance: a turning away from sin and to God, a change of mind so that truth can be perceived. Conversion is a long process for us all, and what pastors do outside the pulpit is crucial here. We are not only preachers. We are also spiritual guides who teach our people, in a multitude of ways, how to grow in Christ and walk in the new life of Spirit-given freedom.

Both in the pulpit and outside it, we must teach our people what it means to be a Christian. This is a long game, not something to tackle in one sermon or one pastoral care session. Nevertheless, over time we can impress on our congregations the truth that Christ gives us an identity that transcends any identities we can give ourselves, while at the same time honoring the distinctives and particularities that make up the dizzying variety of human life. We are black or brown or Indigenous or white, but above all we are God's. And we are made to give our lives to God utterly, and in so doing strengthen the spiritual bond of love between Christ and us and between us and others. In short, the hope for overcoming racism is the same as the hope for overcoming sin, which is the same hope that overcomes death. That hope is Jesus Christ, died and risen and ascended to the Father, who will one day come to judge the living and the dead. Let us never tire of proclaiming that.

Contributors

Raymond Chang is the president of Asian American Christian Collaborative, a pastor, and a writer. He regularly preaches God's word and speaks throughout the country on issues pertaining to Christianity and culture, race, and faith. He has lived throughout the world (Korea, Guatemala, Panama, Spain, China), traveled to over fifty countries, and currently lives in Chicagoland, serving as a campus minister at Wheaton College. Prior to entering vocational ministry, Ray worked in the for-profit and nonprofit sectors, and served in the Peace Corps in Panama. He is currently pursuing his PhD. He is married to Jessica Chang, who serves as the chief advancement and partnerships officer of the Field School.

Daniel Darling is the senior vice president for communications at National Religious Broadcasters. For six years, he served as vice president for communications for the Ethics and Religious Liberty Commission. Dan is a bestselling author of several books, including *Activist Faith*, *The Original Jesus*, *The Dignity Revolution*, and *A Way with Words*. He is the general editor, along with Trillia Newbell, of a small group study on racial reconciliation, *The Church and the Racial Divide*.

J. D. Greear is the pastor of The Summit Church in Raleigh-Durham, North Carolina, and has served as the sixty-second president of the Southern Baptist Convention. He has authored several books, including *Above All, Not God Enough, Gaining by Losing, Gospel, Stop Asking Jesus into Your Heart,* and *Jesus, Continued.* "Summit Life with J. D. Greear" is a daily half-hour radio broadcast featuring his teaching.

J. Daniel Hays is dean of the Pruet School of Christian Studies and professor of Old Testament at Ouachita Baptist University. He earned a ThM from Dallas Theological Seminary and a PhD from Southwestern Baptist Theological Seminary and is the author of *From Every People and Nation: A Biblical Theology of Race, The Message of the Prophets, Jeremiah and Lamentations, The Temple and the Tabernacle,* and *A Christian's Guide to Evidence for the Bible: 101 Proofs from History and Archaeology.* He has also coauthored/coedited *Grasping God's Word, Preaching God's Word, Living God's Word, God's Relational Presence: The Cohesive Center of Biblical Theology, The Baker Illustrated Bible Background Commentary,* and *The Baker Illustrated Bible Handbook.*

Matthew D. Kim is the George F. Bennett Chair of Practical Theology, director of the Haddon W. Robinson Center for Preaching, and director of Mentored Ministry at Gordon-Conwell Theological Seminary in South Hamilton, Massachusetts. He earned a PhD from the University of Edinburgh and is the author of several books, including *Preaching to People in Pain: How Suffering Can Shape Your Sermons and Connect with Your Congregation* (Baker Academic, 2021), *Finding Our Voice: A Vision for Asian North American Preaching* (with Daniel L. Wong, Lexham, 2020), and *Preaching* with Cultural Intelligence: Understanding the People Who Hear Our Sermons (Baker Academic, 2017).

Dhati Lewis is the lead pastor of Blueprint Church in Atlanta and the vice president of Send Network with the North American Mission Board. He completed his undergraduate studies at the University of North Texas, and earned his master's degree from Dallas Theological Seminary and his doctorate of ministry in Great Commission mobilization from Southeastern Baptist Theological Seminary. Dhati has seven beautiful children and is married to Angie, a discerning woman who empowers and encourages him to live fully in his identity in Christ. He is the author of both the Bible study and book Among Wolves: Disciple Making in the City and Advocates: The Narrow Path to Racial Reconciliation.

Bryan Loritts is the teaching pastor of The Summit Church in Raleigh-Durham, North Carolina. He is also the founder and president of the Kainos Movement, an organization committed to seeing the multiethnic church becoming the new normal in our country. He is the author or editor of several books, including Right Color Wrong Culture: The Type of Leader Your Organization Needs to Become Multiethnic and Letters to Birmingham Jail: A Response to the Words and Dreams of Dr. Martin Luther King Jr.

Ray Ortlund is Pastor to Pastors from Immanuel Church in Nashville. He was a founding member of the Council of The Gospel Coalition, serves as the President of Renewal Ministries, and is the author of eight books, including the Preaching The Word commentaries on Isaiah and Proverbs, as well as a contributor to The ESV Study Bible.

The Rt. Rev. **Joey Royal** is a bishop in the Anglican Church of Canada. He currently serves as a suffragan (assistant) bishop in the Diocese of the Arctic, an area that spans 1.5 million square miles of northern Canada. He is also the Director of the Arthur Turner Training School, a theological college that trains Indigenous people for pastoral ministry. He lives in Iqaluit, Nunavut, a small city on Baffin Island, with his wife Jennifer and son Benjamin. He is currently working on his first book, an introduction to worship for Lexham Press's Christian Essentials series.

Juan R. Sanchez serves as senior pastor of the High Pointe Baptist Church in Austin, Texas. In addition to training pastors in the United States, Latin America, South America, and Eastern Europe, he is also a council member of the Gospel Coalition and cofounder and president of Coalición por el Evangelio. Dr. Sanchez serves as recording secretary for the Southern Baptists of Texas Convention and in 2016 was appointed to the faculty of the Southern Baptist Theological Seminary as assistant professor of Christian theology.

Jamaal Williams is the lead pastor of Sojourn Community Church Midtown in Louisville, Kentucky. He is a native of Chicago. Jamaal received a DEdMin from the Southern Baptist Theological Seminary. He also serves as the president of Sojourn Network. Jamaal is married to Amber, and they are the parents of five beautiful children.

Lemanuel Williams is the assistant executive director in an inner-city nonprofit ministry, Peacemakers, in Rocky Mount, North Carolina. Previously, he served as the director of discipleship at Redemption City church in Franklin, Tennessee.

He is a Hunt Scholar completing his Master of Divinity at Southeastern Baptist Theological Seminary.

Jared C. Wilson is assistant professor of pastoral ministry at Spurgeon College, author in residence at Midwestern Baptist Theological Seminary, general editor of *For the Church* (and host of the FTC Podcast), and director of the Pastoral Training Center at Liberty Baptist Church in Kansas City, Missouri.